DEDICATION

In loving memory of my dearest mother, Jean Marie Delaney, who bequeathed to me her love of writing. To my wonderful wife, Anne, in gratitude for her inspiration and all her help along the way.

TABLE OF CONTENTS

PREFACE

In my decades long career, I've had some remarkable and pro-found experiences—some that defy all expectation. In the course of my work, I've been sent to meet with the parents of children who have just died in accidents. I have interviewed a fellow on his deathbed in the hospital one Christmas Eve. (After all, the company that had contracted me always paid well and gave me a lot of business—I prided myself on exchanging value for loyalty.) I once settled a case with a woman who purported to be a witch. I got very bad vibes from her, and I was particularly glad to put some distance between the two of us when all was said and done.

I've met a myriad of characters while on the job. Flamboyance fascinates me and intelligence piques my attention. I have learned something from nearly every person I've encountered, and I've come to one overriding conclusion: greed causes people to behave very poorly. I've seen enough greed to last a hundred life-times. Perhaps I have a somewhat jaded view of human nature, but I prefer to call myself a seasoned cynic. After all, many of the people I have dealt with prove to me, at least, that humans are to be distrusted, though many dispel that notion as well. It is not a paradox. I try to play it one individual at a time, because you never know who might be behind any given door. I don't want to foster the impression that I find people distasteful in a general sense, however. People who have an inner peace are amongst the finest people I've met—they restore my basic faith that all people are inherently good and decent until they prove otherwise.

I interview people for a living, and in many instances, I must convince them to impart information that might not be in their best interest. My calling card says that I am an Investigator and an Adjuster. I am not a private eye, so I don't chase down criminals or handle messy divorce cases, though I was hired once to prove that a fellow was insane so his family wouldn't get stiffed on their inheritance. Mainly, I handle bodily injury cases ranging from automobile crashes to work injuries. Workers compensation, commercial insurance coverage, policies for businesses, and premises liability keep me very busy. I judge situations, and then I advise my client—the insurance carrier what their potential monetary loss might be. I often have the authority to settle cases, so 1 negotiate routinely with attorneys.

Insurance companies expect an adjuster to judge situations and people, and when your job entails meeting a great cross section of the population __ from corporate CEOs to bums on Madison Street _ role-playing is paramount. I have learned the art of adjusting my demeanor to fit the person I am interacting with. I am also obliged to tell my clients, the insurance companies, especially in cases that involve litigation, what type of witness a person I interview will make in front of a jury. Once I can actually get someone to show up for a meeting, he or she almost always open up and speak freely. I have my mother to thank for that _ she taught me how to put people at ease, even if it's just making an initial comment about the weather, or some interest we might share. I always try to start things off with a positive remark to set the tone. I have settled many cases for over six figures, and some in the millions. There is art in finding a middle ground. Some opponents provide reasons for me to be extra competitive in a particular negotiation; I don't mind a good battle. Turning up the heat is particularly satisfying in such instances.

* * *

I have always lived in the Midwest, by the shores of Lake Michigan. The winters are harsh and tedious and seem to last forever, but late spring and summer are delightful, and autumn can be heavenly. There aren't enough superlatives to describe how I feel about my home. I cope with the negative situations

I've been faced with in the last 25 years by embracing the beauty of nature. That, golf, and a sense of humor give me peace in an insane world of juggling multiple tasks, driving all over the Midwest, endless meetings, and the knowledge that most of the people I am meeting with really don't want to talk to me. The fact that the public at large perceives a claims adjuster as a major nuisance doesn't make me think any less of myself at all.

The book that follows is not meant to advise, unless it's a matter of common sense that most people need to be reminded of, nor is the book a work of sociology, philosophy, or ethics. I wrote this book purely because I knew that some of my professional experiences are worth recounting, particularly the humorous ones or the ones that may prove instructive. This has not been an especially cathartic experience, but I have derived a special satisfaction in committing my stories to paper. (Please note: I changed the real names in the stories to protect people's privacy.) Since my early 20s, I have had a strong desire to write. I never pursued or received a PhD, so I consider this my own unique dissertation. My mother, who was a writer herself, bequeathed to me her fascination for words. I hope I can do her proud.

CHAPTER 1: NOVITIATE

When I got out of college, I tried to get a job in sales. Our country was in the midst of a recession, though, and sales jobs were not easy to come by, so I went to work for a national insurance company and absorbed the rudiments of the claims business. I chose insurance work because it was a way to get established and because I was a born salesman endowed with an analytical mind. To be honest, I really didn't know if I would enjoy the work, but I quickly learned that it was something I could do well and I seemed to have the right instincts for dealing with a variety of people, along with ascertaining exactly where their interests lay.

No one ever encouraged me to screw anyone while making a settlement, and a few well-meaning old-timers instructed me to be fair, but not to give the ship away. After about six months, I realized that it was usually best to settle a case for as little as possible. Typically, there are three scenarios. The most common is to find a middle ground everyone can agree on. Unfortunately, there are also a lot people who successfully, and unethically, collect money tax-free—the second scenario. The third scenario is when I find someone who doesn't have dollar signs in his or her eyes; I nip it in the bud on the cheap and get the hell out of there.

Too many cases are compromised because it is almost always cheaper to settle than to pay exorbitant fees to attorneys. Insurance companies benefit when cases are settled reasonably and swiftly—when the lower spectrum of the middle ground is found. When cases are contested, time and money are often wasted; but companies pay people like me quite handsomely when that happens.

Our system is widely abused by greedy, opportunistic people and their attorneys. Insurance companies pay out inordinate sums of money to people whose settlements would be reduced significantly if the case went to trial. In some cases, not-guilty verdicts are the result. Like everything else, legal fees are climbing all the time. Liability policies pay out indemnity dollars, and in most cases defense costs are an additional expense absorbed by the insurance carrier or self-insured entity. A self-insured entity is a corporation or a company that chooses to pay claims out of the corporate till rather than have an insurance carrier provide liability coverage. It is not considered "private insurance," rather a "self-insured retention." Some companies self-insure up to a half million dollars, or even a million dollars, and then they purchase from a carrier an extra- layer insurance coverage to kick in once that money has been exhausted.

In the mid 1970s, I worked for a very large insurance company, which provided me with a nice company car and an expense account. After a week's training in the office, I began receiving claims to investigate and adjust. I had made more money working as a custodian in my college days. Insurance companies and banks have a reputation for paying their non-management people poorly. There have been some great strides in the last 20 to 30 years, but I still believe non-management salaries could be improved significantly. Insurance companies are, on the whole, rather parsimonious, and I believe that they really don't mind a mediocre or lackluster workforce. Management folks are usually fairly sharp and make a decent living, but they are generally not comparable to other managers in private industry. The company I went to work for in the 1970s required that I have a college degree to do claim-adjusting work. It was the people with graduate degrees who could come out of school and demand a higher salary.

My boss there was about 8 years older than I, and he had a huge ego with no substance to back it up. F. Y. Stonewall, a name appropriate for his line of work, was fired six months after I arrived. My next supervisor was a fastidious, meticulous and anal retentive fellow __ the ultimate company man. He was hardworking and highly organized. Naturally, I had much more respect for him than his predecessor, though he possessed an uncanny talent to irritate me. A frustrated middle-management type from the home office arrived about nine months after I start-ed. He declared that he didn't like my work habits and that he was repulsed by my handwriting. As a means of training, I was to write my claims manual answers out in longhand. That's when I realized that my stay at this company would be short-lived. I had, however, learned the fundamentals of the claims business.

My new employer provided liability policies for the city of Chicago and its various departments and governmental agencies. In 1974, one of the first cases I was assigned to involved the Chicago Building Commission and centered around a construction worker who had been working at the bottom of an elevator shaft. Apparently, the fellow had an enemy who had pushed an air compressor down the shaft, hitting him in the back and leaving him a quadriplegic. I took a court reporter with me that day--a gay habitual drunk who proposed marriage to me once in jest. Unfortunately, I had just tied the knot and was unavailable. I inter-viewed all of the workers on the job, and no one claimed to know how the air compressor had dropped. The case was settled in the area of $750,000, and the general contractor was held responsible because they were ultimately responsible for safety on the job site. There had been no barricades surrounding the elevator shaft, which should have been a customary procedure. That was one of my first glimpses into the general laziness and incompetence of the average human being, not to mention the cruelty. I was officially on my way to becoming cynical.

In 1977, I left that company and went to work for two different independent adjusting firms. I knew people who worked for insurance companies and augmented their income by working for independent adjusters on the side. One such fellow made an extra $10,000 over a period of a year. He decided not to report the income and he put down a nice deposit on a home.

My partner of sorts in 1977 was an Irishman named J. J. McGillicuddy. We were introduced by his nephew and hit it off. I called on accounts using his company name, and then we would share the proceeds, though our partnership did not have the benefit of a contract. J.J. McGillicuddy had a fine education. He'd gone to a Jesuit high school and college and was well versed in the classics, including Shakespeare and Chaucer. He not only had a keen awareness and love for the English language, but he also wrote persuasively, and had fine acting skills. His modus operandi was a perfect marriage of substance and blarney. JJ was also so highly motivated; he truly felt that most rules did not apply to him, or that rules were certainly made to be broken. I admired his iconoclastic style. He was the type of person who could talk his way out of anything.

In the early 1950s, JJ had worked for two insurance companies and had enjoyed two company cars and two expense accounts. He was working as an independent adjuster on the side as well. He was exposed when one of his managers called the other manager to chat about a case they shared a mutual interest in. When he mentioned JJ's name, the other fellow declared, "Why, I have a guy working for me by the same name!" After being exposed, J. J. McGillicuddy went into business for himself and became enormously successful.

For me, it was a great relief to escape the rigid and manipulative environment of a large insurance company. In those days, insurance carriers burdened their staff with all manner of paper-work to fill out: 15-day reports, 30-day reports, 45-day reports, and 90-day reports. These procedures made us slaves to our desks, and the act of investigating or adjusting properly was nearly impossible. Though lip service was paid in regard to producing a good work product, the companies seemed to be much more concerned about their employees putting in a 37.5 hour work week. Actual productivity seemed to be secondary.

I also worked with another fellow, Jim Bouska, who provided me with great training and many contacts who served me well. Jim was well known. He had his own company and several employees. I'd heard about him from people I'd worked with at the insurance company. Though he had an explosive temper, he didn't intimidate me, though his other employees quivered in their boots. Between JJ and Jim, I was kept very busy in the late 1970s.

J. J. McGillicuddy worked for a fellow in Freeport, Illinois, whom I'd never met, though I'd spoken to him on the phone on several occasions—he handled the big exposure cases at his company. At the time, my Irish colleague received all of the high impact cases to adjust and to investigate. I'd get a small share, and sometimes we would work together on a case. One such case involved a World War II veteran who had lost both of his feet in the heat of battle. He'd lost one foot to infection, and the other had been blown off by a mine. I called on him after he'd been in an unfortunate accident: he'd been walking across the street, at a major intersection crosswalk at Belmont and Cicero. He was on crutches, and was not crossing against the light. It had been a sunny day. A driver making a left turn claimed he'd never seen him, though, and had mowed him down, breaking his right femur, which is a bone so big it would make a very effective club.

The man ended up at Hines Veterans Administration hospital in Maywood, Illinois. After all he'd been through, I found he'd retained quite a sense of humor. When I arrived to interview him, he insisted on showing me his stubs—I got a close-up view. The poor guy was lonely, and in addition to telling me about the accident, and all the details about his medical attention, he told me his life story. He also confided that his family in Chicago didn't give a hoot about him—he'd never had a visitor in the hospital besides me.

After my meeting, McGillicuddy quizzed me and then called the "guru" of the big case, a fellow at the insurance company who was responsible for monitoring all of the heavy exposure liability cases where there were serious injuries or strong cases of liability against the insured. JJ and the "big gun" decided we could probably settle on the cheap, and I called our claimant, the World War II vet, and arranged a meeting.

In May of 1977, on a Saturday morning, accompanied by my soused court reporter friend, we visited the hospital. Before we arrived, we devised a set of questions that would prove that the footless veteran was perfectly sane and of sound mind. We didn't want anyone to get the impression he didn't know what he was doing by taking $5,000 to settle the case. After he signed the release form, we gave him the check. It was clear he just didn't care about the money, because his case was worth infinitely more. I had not been the decision-maker in this case, but I knew no one would have criticized us for giving him $10,000. Even in 1977, $10,000 would have been a prodigiously small settlement for this type of injury. I felt a pang of guilt, and I thought about the fellow many times. He had stuck to his guns when it came to the issue not being about money, so the result was less heartless than it may appear.

In the following months, I began giving a lot more thought as to how to become more successful in the business. I loved JJ, but his drinking was trouble. I was considering a move out on my own, and I decided that extreme discipline was the answer. I cut down on my drinking and made a major commitment to work. We've all heard about athletes turning it up a notch; that is exactly what I did. Beyond charging less, I also produced high-quality work with concise reports. I never liked overly detailed reports, and I wondered who would have the time to read them. In our industry, we charge by the page for our reports; but overdoing it has a way of coming back to bite you in the ass. During the first three years, I had three accounts feeding me with work on a steady basis. I didn't charge enough, but that made my work steady. This line was very competitive. I worked 70 hours a week on average for the first five years, and I was able to build up a fine following. The late 1980s proved to be smashing success. At my peak, I had six people working for me. Despite my questionable managerial skills, we flourished.

Bouska was still trying to convince me to stay on full-time with him. I played it for what it was worth. Another fellow I'd worked for, Robert Morris, also tried very hard to lure me in. As if resisting a gorgeous woman with bad breath, I had been putting Bouska off. I already worked for him part-time, but he wanted to introduce me to his clients to give them the impression that his business was booming. At a Christmas party, a good friend and business associate of his, Russell Jackson, bragged about all the work he was getting from a new account. The guy was a loud-mouth, especially when drunk. There was no halfway with him. I already knew about the company he was referring to, and because of his loose lips, I was able to get the name of a good contact. I passed the info on to McGillicuddy, and soon we were getting their business on a steady basis. My part-time boss found out and forbade it. I reminded him that I was an independent contractor and there was no conflict of interest, though, and the matter blew over…for a time. Then, the plot thickened.

In the subsequent weeks, his firm had started doing work for the same mutual contact. A month later, he called that mutual contact and informed him that I, indeed, had a broker's license to sell insurance, and that it was entirely possible that I would be stealing business from them. When the work we were getting ground to a halt, I decided it was time to do some explaining. I was able to convince our mutual contact that there was no conflict of interest, and I suggested that he might consider the source of the person who had spread such rumors about my integrity. When it came down to it, Bouska was a first-class prick and a control freak. I'd never had any such problems with McGillicuddy—yet. In hindsight, I suppose it was his way of squashing the competition.

Much of what JJ taught me was invaluable, but by 1978, it was all too apparent that any hope of a protracted collaboration with him was going to be impossible—his drinking was becoming more disruptive and destructive. In fact, his alcoholism had become so severe, he didn't open his mail for two and a half months. Our relationship became very strained at the end—he couldn't, or wouldn't, pay me, as he had burned all his bridges by neglecting his dwindling clientele. I felt I had learned enough to start my own business. I was 29.

A few experiences are emblazoned in my memory from that time. On a warm day in May, before I had opened my own business, I called on a young man at his carpet store in Chicago who had been a passenger involved in a car accident. The driver had been speeding and had crashed. Back then, we wrote our statements in longhand, written in the first person, and we would ask the interviewee to read and sign each page. Perhaps this brash young man hadn't heard me correctly, or maybe he'd chosen not to listen attentively when I informed him that I represented the other driver's insurance carrier. To my amazement, he reported that his friend had been speeding and that they had consumed a couple of beers before getting in the car. I thought I had the goods. He signed the statement and then, with a quizzical look on his face, he had a moment of clarity. As I was putting the statement in the file jacket, he said, "Who did you say you work for?" When I told him, he grabbed the statement and claimed it belonged to him, not me. I tried to reason with him to no avail. I offered him a copy, but he was resolute. On an impulse, I tried to grab it back from him, explaining that once he had relinquished it to me, it was mine and mine alone. The paper ripped and there was a slight struggle, but I wasn't about to give up this damning indictment of his friend, the driver.

I am five foot seven and weigh 150 pounds. This man picked me up and tossed me high over his head onto a role of carpet. I was stunned, and my back hurt. Before I ran out of his store, I called him a few choice names, and then I found a cop and reported the incident. I was told I'd have to go to the station to swear out a complaint. I was not seriously injured, but I was very angry. What disturbed me most was that I wasn't going to be able to deliver the statement to the client in one piece. I still had part of the ripped paper, but that wasn't good enough. Now, we record every interview after receiving consent. My humiliating experience would never have happened had our methods of compiling information been less archaic. Back then a written statement carried more weight in a court of law than a recorded statement. The theory was that a tape could be tampered with.

Later that same year, I had a case involving an old man who had made an illegal left turn and struck two teenagers in a Chevy van. One of them, the passenger, had flown right through the windshield—a veritable human projectile—and ended up in the middle of a major intersection. The glass windshield of the van had not been shatterproof, and had broken out in sheets. The fellow had not been cut badly, but he had a bad case of road rash on his arms, legs and torso. When I went to meet him, I saw that he was still living with his mother. I was taking his statement at the kitchen table when his mother walked in with an odd look on her face. "All you adjusters are the same!" she blurted out before beating me over the head with a rolled-up newspaper. She had wide gaps in her teeth and she sprayed me with saliva as she pummeled me. Her son, being the compassionate fellow that he was, suggested we finish our business at a local Burger King. He must have felt sorry for me because he settled his case for $750 on the spot it was worth a least $5,000. Although I didn't find it funny at the time, it's a knee slapper in retrospect.

I was still working with JJ in 1979, and we were sharing expenses on a particular account. But JJ wouldn't show me the billing. We had a lunch set up at a nice Italian place with a new contact, but JJ got drunk and didn't show up for the meeting. I didn't have a credit card at that time, but he did. Our arrangement had been that he would charge the lunch, and 1 would reimburse him for half. I didn't have enough cash to pay the bill. In fact, I didn't even have my wallet with me. When I called him in desperation, I was astounded he actually answered the phone. He was unapologetic. "You take care of it," he said. I thought for a couple of minutes and realized I was being used, both figuratively and literally. I'd had it. So I simply walked out of the place, left our new contact at the table, with no explanation whatsoever. I called McGillicuddy and told him what I'd done. He thought it was uproariously funny. When I got to Bouska's office that afternoon, he'd already heard the story and felt it necessary to chastise me.

I worked for yet another guy for a short time—a hell of a character. He told me he'd once been caught by his wife at a motel in broad daylight. She'd driven by and recognized his car—it was the only one in the lot, and he had a baby-blue Olds Toronado. When he finished relating the story, he said, "I don't think my wife trusted me much after that, but boy was it worth it. Just remember, son, when you settle a case with a beautiful woman, or any woman, don't have a sexual liaison with her until a month after the settlement."

It was also around that time that I had to begin learning when to say "go" and when to say "no" something I would struggle with for the rest of my career. Some people don't know how to finish anything. I am a finisher, but there has to be something in it for me. Sometimes, I carry it too far. I went too far in a south-side Chicago neighborhood in late 1980 to see a lady at 71st and Princeton on a case. She knew I was coming, but it remains a mystery as to whether she set me up. Four men attacked me with a knife and robbed me of my wallet and $35. They left me with my keys and briefcase. It happened in the lobby of her apartment building as I was searching for the right buzzer to ring—vandals had scratched all the names away. Regardless, I interviewed the woman while I waited for the police to come. I got what I came for, even if the bad guys got the best of me.

My mood was jocular on a fine May day in 1980 when I took some special people to lunch. They had helped put me on the map, business-wise. One fellow was a good friend and a real clown. He also had a serious side, though, and he was a fine technician as a claims professional. We went to a place called Orlando's on Wells Street, which was right around the corner from their office—a casual establishment with a bar for those who liked to drink their lunch. As we sat around the table, Joe asked for two of my new business cards. He looked at them for a moment and then ripped them up. He threw them on the table and said, "This is what we think about your company." I was dumbstruck, but all of the other men laughed heartily. I hoped he was just kidding around. Before lunch, he'd handed me a couple of new cases to work on. Was this guy putting me on or was he nuts? Our relationship would develop into a long lasting friend-ship and business association. I worked with his company until 1987, when they had a change of management.

In my first year of business on my own, I opened exactly 100 cases. I was on cloud nine. Up until January of 1981, I had contracted out with one other company, but after that, I was entirely on my own. My strategy? I'd undercut the competition from a price standpoint; despite my youthful looks and perceived lack of experience, those I called on almost had to consider using me based on price alone. Doors opened quickly. I was single at the time, I didn't really have any great overhead, I did not own a house, and I had fairly simple tastes at that point.

For me, the risk was minimal— there was no way I was going back to work for a company or for someone who wouldn't pay me commensurate to my skill. I really had nowhere else to go. It's like that "Me and Bobby McGee" song: "Freedom's just another word for nothing left to lose." I worked out of my home until June of 1985, and then I found a sublet at Touhy and Harlem in Chicago. I had about 350 square feet to start with, but we grew. The owner of the building and I became golfing pals and I joined his club. I'm still there today. I entertained a lot of clients there, and 1 used it to enhance the appearance of my business. It's also a place, to this day, where I can unwind; it helps to preserve my sanity after dealing with people who sometimes rub me the wrong way.

Back then, I had a prevailing feeling that I was either very lucky or extremely blessed. I knew, though, that it wasn't pure luck that generated my success. It was also incredible drive and energy, and the perspicacious talent I had to pounce on opportunities. Being aggressive and stubborn took me a long way, although it got me into trouble periodically. Not only was I lucky, but I also felt the timing seemed to work out very well. I was able to find people who were willing to give a relatively inexperienced person some trust, and above all, continued work. I'm a finisher, and a lot of what I did was based on being very tenacious and not taking rejection the wrong way. There was also an anger factor that drove me to be successful. Some of that stemmed from doubters, and my number-one doubter was probably my father. I never held that against him, but it really prompted me to show him that I was going to be very successful in spite of his skepticism.

In 1985, after taking a lot of work as an independent contractor for a certain company for five solid years, they pulled the plug. I had poured a lot of sweat into producing results far and above the ordinary for them, and then the owner died and left the company to his daughter, who did not understand the first thing about the business. Within nine months, she had engineered its sale. Part of the agreement was that she remain on as a principal and board director. She was ousted two years later. When the new regime came in, they immediately began to look at expenses. Naturally, they decided they were paying too much for independent adjuster fees. I had gotten the business initially because I charged 20 percent less than the competition. They did not have any outside adjusters, and one reason for their success was that they had been able to control the outflow of indemnity dollars. Indemnity dollars equate to money that insurance companies pay out for settlements. They are different from expense dollars, but they all come from the same corporate till.

By my account, I had saved them at least $2 million. I got to people quickly, I held their hands, and I kept them away from attorneys, eventually settling their claims. A little attention went a long way. I settled claims for peanuts for them. An inference was made, though, that I was paying a percentage of my earnings to lock up the work. The inference was made by management, and I couldn't confirm it, but it had to be the daughter of the owner, who was by then an officer of the corporation and was determined to put her own imprint on it. Their allegation, in other words, was that I was paying kickbacks to the claims manager. All I can say is that it was untrue. I had developed quite a rapport with him—we would go to lunch once a month; at Christmas time, I would buy him a gift to show my appreciation. Our relationship was friendly, but that was the extent of it. I deeply resented the inference, and I could see that both of us were out with this new management. I had been their number-one vendor handling claims; it was the first real business loss I'd suffered and it hit me hard. At least I got paid.

Being Irish, I have an excellent memory. In September of 1985, after our relationship had been severed for three months, I received a call commanding me to testify for a case I had worked on for them involving an insured who failed to cooperate in a claim investigation after a loss. They wanted me to testify that I had made every effort to garner his cooperation and to present the history of his case. The insurance company had filed a declaratory action against the uncooperative insured, which was a violation of the policy language and agreements. In essence, the carrier was asking the court to approve and sanction the carrier's attempt to void coverage, based on the cooperation clause in the policy. All liability policies have language spelling out the duties that an insured has after a loss occurs. The language in the policy mandates that the insured give full cooperation to the insurance carrier to aid them in the collection of pertinent information.

I was not enthusiastic about the fact that I was being compelled to testify on their behalf, so I told their defense counsel that we would have to have an upfront agreement about what I was to be paid for my services. They were most disagreeable when I told them it would cost $500 a day, because they were depriving me of my livelihood. They balked. The next thing I knew, they had issued a subpoena. The message was loud and clear: I would testify and capitulate, or I would become a hostile witness. I decided at the last minute not to show. The owner's daughter called and threatened me. I told her point blank that I could play hardball, too. The insurance company's attorney called to tell me that the judge wanted to cite me for contempt of court. He'd begged the judge not to issue the order. 1 repeated my terms and told the defense attorney that if they wanted me to testify without payment, I would act as a hostile witness with a failed memory. The owner's daughter was too proud to work out a compromise. In the end, I was not cited for contempt—which would have meant a fine and jail time. The insurance company lost the declaratory action and had to pay the claim. It cost the company $25,000 to settle. It would have cost them $500 to have me testify and help them win the declaratory action against the insured. If you multiply $500 times 50, that comes out to $25,000.

CHAPTER 2: OVERVIEW

Day in and day out, I handle people's dirty laundry. The trade-off is that I am paid commensurately for that privilege. The message I have always conveyed is one of opportunity. It's not always the way I feel, but role-playing is essential in drumming up business. Truth can sometimes be elusive, and perception is as valuable as truth, I've found. In many cases, they overlap. Putting on a positive front at all times for your clients is a must. Negativity does not sell well. I am an optimist, and I believe I can win every time out. I'm not blind to mistakes, however. I have learned to adjust.

I once asked a client when he wanted a job completed. He jokingly told me he wanted it done yesterday. I knew he was joshing, but he could do that in the best relationships. One of the best relationships I ever enjoyed in the insurance industry was in the early days with a company called Ohio Casualty, from 1980 to 1987. We formed a strong and long-lasting relationship. These were serious claims people who were treated like professionals by management, as opposed to a necessary evil. In the industry, claims people are perceived as bad guys, mostly, who spend hard-earned premium dollars. Most property-casualty companies, even in the 21st century, still subscribe to that negative theory, either subconsciously or overtly. The pervasive attitude is that the claim professional is the scourge of the industry because we give away money needlessly, thereby diluting profit margins. This is manifested by the bipolar shifts in philosophy regarding the handling of procedures when dealing with claims: Insurance carriers in the liability business hire a mountain of people, and then when business slows down, they lose people, mainly by attrition. This particular approach correlates with regular business cycles. Other philosophical shifts include paying out claims like crazy, sometimes to the point of overpaying, simply to get them off the books.

Reserves are not assets for an insurance company; rather, a reserve is money set aside to represent the potential value of a claim. Companies, in the course of 12 months, may go from the "overpay philosophy" to the "underpay method," which makes the books look better in the short term. My personal moniker for this activity is the "let's play the accumulation of litigated files game"

A well-run company has very strict underwriting procedures before they will accept a risk. They look at the risk and evaluate a number of factors before they decide what premium to charge. Some insureds will go to a company with less stringent under-writing procedures and therefore be charged a lesser premium for the coverage.

A well-run property-casualty company tries to avoid the "litigated files game" because legal fees do not reduce liability limits. In other words, in the instance where a policy has a million-dollar liability limit, even if the company has a one-million dollar exposure on a loss, the company is still obliged to pay legal fees, even though they may have to pay the entire policy limit. This would be reflective of an extreme instance, but if a case is potentially worth a million dollars, the legal fees can easily run in the six-figure range.

Because business is more cutthroat than ever before, management, generally speaking, seems to have a very negative attitude about claims professionals. Short-term expectations on Wall Street foster quick fixes and schizophrenic responses to changing markets. Some companies chase business, which brings in immediate gratification with premium dollars; but there is always a day of reckoning. The gnashing of teeth begins when multiple claims mushroom out of control. The best organizations, including Chubb and American International Group (AIG), who are in the property-casualty business, attempt to resist chasing the market; they stick to a conservative approach.

Anyone who ever sat in an army or police department roll call knows how claim professionals feel. There are a lot of hindsight experts—Monday morning quarterbacks—out there. Insurance companies have been guilty of overworking their claims people, creating strained relationships. A negative environment is borne of claims professionals feeling like second-class citizens, pariahs, even. While it's true that salaries have risen dramatically over the years for my colleagues, I would personally be in the funny farm by now if I had continued working for a carrier. As an independent, I feel some negativity too, but I have freedom of movement, I can stomach the fallout. Hell, I can even find a way to put a positive spin on it!

Negotiations and Psychology

Over the years, I've been called upon to settle cases by insurance carriers who realize that as a professional, I know my market-place. This includes knowing intrinsically what a case is worth. Knowing your adversary helps, but it is not necessary. I must also be able to assimilate much information before making a recommendation to secure the authority to settle a case. Some of the most delicate dealings to resolve a matter take place between me, as the intermediary, and the company issuing the authority. The carrier, in certain instances, needs to be assuaged, cajoled, and directed, amongst other creative tactics. Some companies make a business decision and give me, the independent adjuster, a one-time opportunity to settle. In essence, they tell me to either settle for the amount we have authorized or less, or close the file. I call it a "line of demarcation."

Knowing your market means knowing the attorneys with whom you are negotiating. Again, this is not essential, but it doesn't hurt when you know what to expect. I try to personalize conversations to make for a more pleasant experience, and that has been a great aid in loosening lips. The negotiation process doesn't have to be akin to pulling teeth, unless the other side is intractable. I always attempt to channel a conversation so that we can both participate comfortably. I'll bring up sports, a hobby, children, or current events. I slide in and out of the subject matter until we have had enough discussion about the issue at hand, and then I begin to summarize why I have made an offer. I never give away the limit of my authority immediately, unless my authority is so limited that offering less would be counterproductive, or downright silly.

I settled a case recently for $11,500. The initial demand from the attorney was $30,000. I generally feel that an attorney is foolish to put forth a conservative demand, because if an attorney asks for a very generous amount, they never know who might just say yes. Asking for a substantial amount allows more room to maneuver. Most of these settlement discussions are done by telephone; rarely are they conducted in person, particularly when it involves an attorney and an adjuster.

For me, the satisfaction I derive from my work involves two things. The first is orchestrating a great investigation that allows a case to be denied with little or no chance for the other party to recoup anything. The second is negotiating a favorable settlement for the company, whether it is self-insured or an insurance carrier. Most defense lawyers and insurance company claim professionals recognize an excellent result. This helps someone like me to garner more business. When I settle a case favorably, I can charge for rendering my expertise. Getting excellent results on a consistent basis makes me feel like I am doing something inherently worthwhile.

It always amazes me that so many people are unaware of the fact that they don't have to report money accepted in an insurance settlement as income, and therefore no taxes are owed. I use this constantly in settlement negotiations as a means of selling the true value of the settlement. On many occasions, just the mention of this concept has made the settlement offered seem more attractive. Also, during settlement negotiations, I never talk about reimbursing gross wages. I always talk about net income. If a person was working at the time of the accident and had lost income, they certainly don't take home gross wages, but net wages. This concept has served me well. Attorneys will argue that in a court of law they consider gross wages and not net income. I remind them that we are not negotiating in a court of law, and we are not bound by those restrictions. If you are dealing with an attorney who truly feels that he can secure a lot more money for himself and his client, you will find that they will not spend much time haggling over a perceived low-ball offer on a case. Instead, the attorney will file suit and raise the stakes.

If suit is filed, many, but not all carriers have house counsel who will defend. They are already on the payroll, so there are no extraordinary expenses right away as regards litigation. However, in some instances, carriers will not have house counsel handle a case because they are overloaded; they send the matter to an out-side defense attorney. The meter starts running right away, usually at least at $125 to $175 an hour. The money expended for an outside attorney affects the bottom line for that carrier as much as paying out settlement dollars, but it is easier to quantify expense dollars. It is far more difficult to quantify settlement dollars because every case has its own merits, and there is no set formula or criteria for settling cases.

It's pretty easy to tell if an attorney is willing to settle or not. They won't be as impatient as an attorney who is not going to spend much time mulling over an offer lacking real punch from their perspective. I have actually seen attorneys short shrift their clients for one reason or another -it depends a lot on the attorney's cash flow. However, I have never had an attorney tell me that his cash flow was lousy. There have been a couple of cases where I sensed that they'd taken less, just to secure the check. Most attorneys take a third of the award if the case is settled short of filing suit, or 40 percent if the case goes to trial. This is done by contract with the client. In a minor's case, the attorney usually ends up taking a third. On a worker's compensation case, the attorney will take a lesser percentage.

When they start asking questions about how soon we can deliver the check, I begin to wonder about their financial situation. When I sense the attorney is locked into settling, rather than filing suit, I try to press and squeeze for an advantageous settlement for the carrier. I am trying to justify my own worth or job existence. If I make the person who hires me look smart, maybe he or she will hire me on a repeat basis.

Not only do I carefully look for an advantage with attorneys, but also with individuals. Attorneys are actually easier to deal with in most respects than laymen, because they know values and they know how to negotiate. People, in many instances, get advice from friends, family, neighbors, fellow claims adjusters, or lawyers who would not take the case because they predominantly practice law in other fields. They still dispense advice, whether expert or not.

Years ago, I had a case where a pedestrian was hit by a truck. The records at the hospital suggested that the victim suffered a seizure as a result of the physical trauma. I could not find any-thing to suggest to the contrary. The attorney sent the damages, and we negotiated for three weeks. The initial demand was $64,000, and I offered $10,000. We eventually settled the case for $16,500, though I'd been given $30,000 in authority. The attorney must have known that the seizure issue was not as cut and dried as he wanted me to believe, because he came down dramatically from the $64,000 demand so readily. I surmised that if they felt the seizure issue was so powerful that they could have held out for more, or filed suit, then they would have done so. I suspected that person was having seizures before the accident. Essentially, I called their bluff.

There is a parallel between a hard-fought negotiation and playing a game of cards. Of course, the concept of who blinks first applies to some degree, but when negotiating, there isn't the specter of physical harm, only mental anguish. Mental anguish comes into play when you have a case evaluated at a certain dollar value, or a range of value. When you offer the lowest end of the spectrum from a value standpoint, your opponent says without hesitation, "Sure, we'll take it!" Then you begin to wonder if perhaps you've evaluated the case improperly. At that point, you want to kick yourself for not offering a lower amount. But that happens about as frequently as a

Chicago baseball team winning the World Series. The reverse is much more common: you offer the low end of the range, and the adversary responds as if you've lost your marbles: "How can you insult me like that?" is the common response, or, "I'd never consider anything like that!" Usually, in these situations, I retort that I was under the impression that justice takes precedence over money. That gives them something to contemplate. Typically, this takes place during face-to-face meetings with a third-party claimant, but on occasion, attorneys feign bruised feelings, too.

Usually, attorneys are not so easily insulted. They just feign insult to mask their greed. Ninety-nine times out of a hundred, I settle cases where a low offer meets with resistance. Most people who engage an adjuster on a one-to-one basis don't particularly like attorneys, and they don't want to see an attorney take a third of the settlement. They are street smart enough to recognize that they can benefit by securing more money that way. An insurance carrier knows the value of a case, attorney or no attorney, so settling with an individual for a little more than that person would realize if they'd hired an attorney, but less than the carrier would pay by avoiding the attorney's fee, makes for a decent settlement.

In my capacity, I have saved carriers hundreds of thousands of dollars by arranging for an extension of time to make an appearance, and file an answer regarding numerous lawsuits. This buys the carrier time to pursue settling a case without incur-ring legal expenses. It also gives the plaintiff's attorney time to put together a package of damages such as medical bills, records and verification of lost income. If we can settle a case reason-ably, it is usually done within the time allotted, or we might even arrange for an additional extension of time to answer the lawsuit. On occasion, I have arranged for more time with which to answer a suit after the initial allotted period of time is expended. Typically, I will ask for a 90-day extension of time to answer, whether there is service or not on the person that the insurance carrier would be obliged to defend. In a couple of instances, I have arranged for extensions for an entire year. It is very rare when a judge will step in and force the carrier to hire council. As long as the carrier and the plaintiff attorney are trying to work out a resolution, judges usually do not intervene.

In all instances when I have met with people to settle cases face to face, I throw out an offer—less than I am prepared to pay. I look them square in the eye when consternation is evident on their faces, which is usually within five or ten seconds, meaning I have offered less than they think they deserve. I let them sit and contemplate this while I look down at my shoes. I must say a typically awkward moment. In the vast majority of cases, we resolve the matter right then and there for either the amount proposed initially, or for another hundred dollars or so. Occasionally, I'll get a hold-out who will eventually settle after a few phone calls subsequent to the initial face-to-face meeting. The releases are sent through the mail, and eventually it sinks into everyone's cranium that no more money is on the table. In most cases, settling is the prudent thing to do. Most people don't want to go through the hassle of hiring an attorney, and few people actually trust attorneys.

Usually, if an attorney is involved in a case, he or she has been hired before I take the assignment. Every once in a while, a person I have contacted, someone whom I have already taken a statement from regarding the facts and their injuries, will develop cold feet and hire an attorney. In Illinois, the statute of limitations is two years for an adult. This means they have two years to settle the case or file a lawsuit to keep their claim alive. Some states have statutes of limitations greater than two years. In a medical malpractice action, the statute is predicated on the discovery of the problem or illness. In product liability cases in Illinois, after ten years, a manufacturer cannot be held accountable for a defect in a product. We call this the statute of repose.

An attorney called me once, asking for an offer on a case. My response was $20,000 as it was a particularly bad injury—a fractured fibula with clear-cut negligence on the part of the insured. The attorney accused me of rendering a low-ball offer. He said he would fix it with my principal so that they would not give me any more work, and he intimated that I was a lousy negotiator—that I did not negotiate in good faith. Then he called me every name in the book. It's hard to respond because of his tirade, so I told him to call me when his hemorrhoids weren't acting up. Perhaps we could have a reasonable conversation at that point. This was an attorney I'd run across before, when he'd asked me how much I was willing to offer after we'd secured the medical records demonstrating that his client had fallen on a patch of ice rather than falling down the common stairway in his apartment building. We'd settled the matter for $21,500, though I'd had $24,000 in authority. He didn't have to know that. There was no way that my principal would give any credence to his opinion about my adjusting or investigative abilities, so not for a moment did he cause me any trepidation. I think he was just testing me to see if I could be intimidated. He knew before his tirade that it was unlikely, and yet he tried the ploy anyway. He was known to be an ill-tempered fellow, and he was likely blowing off steam.

As the years went by, I ended up settling quite a few cases with this fellow, and I always felt that these settlements were advantageous to my side. We also talked a good deal about golf, and he frequently invited me to his country club. I kept on telling him that I wasn't interested, and furthermore, I couldn't afford to let it get out publicly that I was cavorting with him. I did tell him once that my wife and I would like to see his house in Highland Park, and without hesitation, he invited us for dinner. His house, recently built, was the subject of a flattering article in the Chicago Tribune, complete with color photos. According to the paper, one of its outstanding features was a 50- by-15 foot indoor pool with ornate tile around the perimeter. During the day, the grand pool had natural solarium lighting, and a complicated array of overhead lighting kicked in at night. Later, I told him I was just kidding about seeing his house, and we never look him up on his offer. I'm not sure that he was really serious anyway, though he made it clear that it was an open invitation. I'll bet he would have loved to gain some leverage over me to use in any future negotiations. I had no intention of giving him any.

Some cases settle with the first meeting; others take months. Usually, the smaller settlements go by the boards—they're the quickest but not always. The biggest and nastiest problems in my experience have occurred on property damage cases rather than bodily injury cases. Sometimes we're talking about an $800 award, and the claimant simply refuses to compromise! When they start calling the company and demanding to speak to the higher-ups, when they start annoying the executives, it's amazing how quickly they get satisfaction, though. The squeaky wheel gets the most grease, I guess.

And have no doubt about it—people get nasty on a regular basis. On one occasion, I made a settlement with a fellow regarding a damaged roof at his place of business. We made a compromised settlement because he already had some prior damage to the same area. While I was exchanging the check and having the releases signed, two of my tires were mysteriously punctured. He must have subscribed to the theory, "Don't get mad, get even."

Substandards

One substandard ploy is to interpret coverage issues with the notion of not providing coverage. Business is conducted on the premise that not all insurance companies in the property-casualty field operate alike. The good companies have some commonalities: they hire honest people who put forth professionalism. The higher up the ladder an adjuster rises, the more prevalent the professional attitude becomes. There are also companies who operate on the edge—this is manifested by their refusal to pay third- party claims until they're forced to by judgment. These are known in the business as "substandards," and they specialize in screwing policy holders out of their coverage. They are experts at finding loopholes to deny or reduce coverage.

Generally, companies of this nature look for any opportunity to deny coverage. Sadly, this leaves the policyholder in a difficult and unfair position —one of fending for oneself. This state of affairs is allowed to continue because the Department of Insurance refuses to exercise its broad power to stop this activity. The Illinois Department of Insurance (IDI) has the power to make life very difficult, or even to shut down the substandard insurance carriers. They don't do it at all because the major carriers don't mind that the substandards take a lot of the unenviable risks that major carriers don't want. Basically, that's why they are allowed to remain in business and operate on the "fringe" of the rules and regulations set forth by the IDI. The IDI has the power to do whatever they want to the substandards, but they don't exercise that power because the major carriers don't want them to. The key is substandards have to maintain proper reserves, similar to a bank. There is a very strong insurance lobby in the state of Illinois, and also on a federal level. The large insurance companies have a lot of clout and pay a lot of money to the attorneys that are in the various legislatures. Consequently, our courts are continuously clogged with cases that the substandards should have been paid and settled long ago without the court's involvement. This mess is promoted by not paying third-party claims and letting them go into suit.

Better carriers don't seem to mind, because these substandards take the many insureds who carry high-risk factors. Even today, there are still at least a million people in the Chicago area driving without insurance, though the state has a mandatory law requiring it. As is the case in all matters of law, one is innocent until proven guilty. It is not necessary to provide proof of insurance coverage when license plates are procured.

Substandard carriers do not limit themselves to automobile coverage. Many also write homeowner's coverage and some small business risks, including dram shop or liquor liability. Any establishment that sells or serves liquor must purchase dram shop liability. It is mandatory. This protects not only the establishment, but also an innocent third party that might be injured by someone who was drinking at that establishment, or someone who bought liquor at that establishment.

I once worked for a substandard that aspired to respectability in the early 1980s. I made a nice buck doing business with them, and I continued on there for about three years, because they paid their bills on time. At that juncture in my career I was just getting established. I worked for this particular company because I needed the work and I needed the money. They were making an effort to establish a more respectable business practice, and I decided to judge their ethics mostly by whether they paid my bills on time. They were pretty good at that, so I stayed with them until they were liquidated three years later.

This company wrote a fair degree of commercial insurance, and they were eventually bought out by Berkshire-Hathaway, owned by Warren Buffet. Fantastic sums of money were pumped into their Illinois operation so that they could gain market share and upgrade their image. Prior to this infusion of capital, their books reflected that they had written several high-crime area properties, which generated multiple claims. But they had no one on their staff to go out and investigate these claims. As a result, I found myself going off to some fairly dangerous locations. Naturally, I was as careful as possible, but I couldn't help but wonder if it was worth the effort.

One policy they wrote was for a building at 40th and Indiana, in Chicago. I traveled there on a Saturday morning in June of 1983 to investigate a rat bite case. The building in question was insured by my principal, the insurance company, and one of the tenants had been bitten as he was talking on the telephone to his girlfriend. The rat had jumped up on his bed and sunk its teeth straight through his jeans and onto his thigh. The gentleman described the rodent as being the size of a cat. He'd gone to the emergency room and had incurred a bill for $100. I settled the case for $175.

While I was there, the man's grandfather told me that on a summer evening at dusk, there were usually 20 to 30 large rats on top of the refrigerator and kitchen table. With this news, and the knowledge that I didn't want to be there when the sun was going down, I beat it out of there fast.

Birdie or Bogey

Over the years, I have, by necessity or from pleasure, mastered the most important part of my career: creativity and thinking out-side the box. When fraud's afoot, it's very hard to hide it from me. Until 1994, an independent adjuster could legally perform surveillance without a private detective's license in the state of Illinois. I always despised that type of work---it was very tedious sitting for hours twiddling my thumbs before even catching the scent of the desired subject. With plenty of time to think, 1 figured out a way to expose a business owner who maintained that his life had been ruined by an automobile accident. His MRI suggested that he had two herniated disks. Furthermore, he had taken a blow to his head, which had destroyed his equilibrium. I never saw his car, but it had apparently been a total loss. I tried to identify him at his place of business doing something strenuous, but I couldn't catch him lifting any boxes or doing any jumping jacks.

In his deposition, the man claimed that his golf game had gone to hell after the accident. Coincidentally, I had a friend who served on the board of the Chicago District Golf Association. The injured claimant belonged to a club in Wisconsin that was an associated member club of the Chicago District, so we decided to check his name. Sure enough, our computer search came up with results. We were even able to get his golf scores two years before the accident, and two years after the accident. For about six months after the accident, which had occurred during the winter, he'd posted no golf scores at all. Then, he'd started to play regularly. Lo and behold, he had actually shaved three strokes off his handicap in the last two years!

The defense attorney took the case to trial and exposed the would-be suffering golfer as an abject liar. Though he'd stated in his deposition that he hadn't even had the desire to play golf after the accident, he'd posted more than 75 eighteen-hole rounds in a year's time! The jury didn't take well to the new information. They gave him nothing for trying to cheat the system. This fellow had run afoul of an all too common trap ____ greed. But he didn't get away with it.

It also pays to scrutinize records carefully. In many instances, records will reveal a possible intervening cause of a claimed injury. When a claimant suffers an accident and is injured, it is sometimes possible that the injury is not, in fact, new. In many cases the initial injury has healed by the time a new accident occurs, and a new fictitious injury is blamed on the accident fraudulently. Or, an old injury may simply be exacerbated by an event after the accident has occurred, prolonging discomfort and the need for medical attention. Intervening causes can include a fall in the shower, a sports injury, an automobile accident, or an injury at work. It can also be an old-fashioned beating.

In times past, one could saunter into the medical records department of a hospital and immediately have a look. If you found something notable, you could have it copied right there on the spot. Depending on how voluminous the files were, you could have them copied in five or ten minutes for a modest fee. Now, most hospitals have copy services and provide no instant gratification. Sometimes, a 24-hour notice is required. You can only view records with a current authorized consent form signed by the patient.

I walked into Illinois Masonic Hospital in November of 1984 with an authorization form signed by a patient; I had the records in less than 15 minutes. It cost the insurance company $15, plus my time. This inquiry had been prompted by an infamous ambulance-chasing attorney who had presented a claim for a fellow with a broken ankle. The allegation was that he had fallen down the common stairway in his apartment building because the carpeting was loose, and because the wooden step under the carpet was broken. They even had photos. They forwarded me a consent form and I called to ask who the treating doctor was. They gave me the name of an orthopedic doctor, but conspicuous in its absence was any mention of the client going to an emergency room. The bill from the doctor suggested that the client had first seen the doctor two days after the date of the accident. This immediately raised a red flag.

I knew where the claimant lived, and I spent two hours on the phone calling ten north-side area hospitals. Finally, I hit on the right one. Illinois Masonic Hospital had the records. I was over there in 20 minutes. The records they had corresponded to the accident date. Sure enough, this fellow had never fallen down a stairway __ he'd told the hospital that he'd fallen on an ice patch while crossing the street.

When I got back to my office, I called the attorney and told him the bad news. He didn't really appear to be too surprised. He put me on the phone with the head of the firm, who had the cojones to ask how much we were willing to pay. I retorted that unless they withdrew from the case, I would call the Attorney Registration Disciplinary Commission and wage a complaint. I received a letter from the attorney two days later withdrawing from the case. Ironically, the lying patient called me and begged me to reconsider, complaining that he had to pay the doctor. He said it was all a monumental misunderstanding.

Claims professionals occasionally leave their ethics behind and cavort with the plaintiff's bar to get kickbacks on settlements. I personally know at least three claims professionals who have been implicated in scams with attorneys involving kickbacks, or having false invoices sent to files and then paying the invoices. The plaintiff's bar represents a plaintiff or a claimant in a civil suit against a party that they feel has wronged them in some way. This is called a tort. Civil suits are different from criminal matters—the burden of proof is less onerous in a civil suit.

Sometimes insurance professionals will take money from the plaintiff's bar in the form of a kickback and part of the scheme is that they can pay the plaintiff's attorney even more money on a case than normal. It is a matter of one hand washing the other. This is indubitably illegal, and as heinous as a crooked judge. For me, it's something of a curiosity—in my mind, it's simply not worth it when there are so many honest ways to make money. Even blatantly dishonest people I have known were offered new jobs almost immediately when they were fired for fraudulent misbehavior. Employers usually refuse to prosecute and have been hesitant to give flat-out, unadulterated, unmitigated bad references. Ya still gotta look in the mirror, though.

An Egregious Oversight

Most of the court cases I've been involved with, either directly or indirectly, have been heard in the Circuit Court of Cook County. They were preeminently law division cases or cases in the municipal court, which now has a $30,000 cap. There are several municipal courts in the outlying areas of Cook County. As a rule, Du Page County juries are extremely conservative. I have on occasion seen attorneys ask for a transfer to a federal court in order to escape the wrath of the citizens of Du Page. Cook is famous for crooked politicians _________ the city of Chicago is in Cook County, and Cook is well known for very liberal juries in civil cases.

In the 1990s, I was called for jury duty in Du Page County. The case involved an insurance agent who had not turned in the premiums belonging to a man who had died. The insurance company refused to voluntarily pay the death benefit, so the policy holder's family sued both agent and company. My own feeling was that if I had waited for three months without satisfaction (meaning no forthcoming policy), I'd be all over the agent.

During jury selection, one of the questions was: "How do you feel about insurance companies?" I gave them the most flippant answer I could think of, because I couldn't afford to get tied up on a jury for any great length of time. I was hoping they would dismiss me. I answered: "They're okay if they pay their bills on time." The attorneys already knew what I did for a living. I was immediately dismissed.

CHAPTER 3: FRAUD

Unscrupulous people are pervasive in our society and, naturally, the insurance industry seems to be a magnet for people wanting to commit fraud. Here's a tip: One of the safest ways to rip some-one off it is to instigate fraud with an insurance company. People have tried countless ways to pull a fast one for money—they pad the list of items they claim have been stolen; they stay off work for an extra week to pad an injury claim; they'll have a carrier fix a car for a "pre-existing" condition. These are all minor league. But there are more grandiose schemes to bilk your friendly insurance carrier, too.

Attorneys play a big part when it comes to bilking insurance companies. They can be patently unscrupulous and downright disingenuous when it comes to bringing a claim on behalf of a client. Most attorneys who handle personal injury cases are legitimate, the majority of the time. The ones who use the same medical providers over and over are typically in cahoots with doctors.

The more recent efforts of State Farm and Allstate have made it increasingly difficult to perpetuate these types of scams. They've acted as watchdogs, protecting the industry's reputation and fighting back against the fraud-mongers. The main auto insurers simply are not voluntarily paying out "soft tissue" injury claims that are inflated because of bloated medical bills and questionable lost-income claims. Many auto claims resulting from little or no impact are not winning large sums anymore. As regards auto cases with very light or non-existent impacts, carriers used to pay out pretty good money to settle. Typically, those were rear-end accidents. When you rear end someone's car, it's akin to absolute liability—then it becomes a question of dam-ages. There were, and still are, a lot of lawyers that will abuse these types of cases and direct clients to doctors that will run up bills and tell people to stay off work for longer than medically necessary. State Farm and Allstate are the principal leaders in the fight against this type of abuse, and they have set a new tone for the industry in not overpaying these types of claims.

The most-often repeated advice I hear regarding bodily injury cases is the "three times" rule. A good example is a person with $2,000 in medical bills, and with a good case of negligence against the wrongdoing party. This has to be a situation with no permanent injuries, however. In the industry, we call it a "bump and bruise" case. The claimant is told to fight for $6,000, though I will probably offer them $4,000. In this situation, there is no attorney involved. I'll probably go as high as $4,500 or $4,750, if absolutely necessary. The "three times" rule is terribly misconstrued these days. Some 20 or 25 years ago, it was much more common. The formula works as follows; the medical bills get paid, an equal amount goes to the client and the attorney gets an equal amount for his or her fee. If carriers typically settled all cases of this nature for three times the bills accrued, then they wouldn't need a human being to negotiate! I have settled many cases based on the "three times" rule, but I always look at each case individually. If it is a "bump and bruise" case, the "three times" rule, if the medical bill amount is small, may be appropriate.

The property-casualty business now has a new weapon used to help evaluate bodily injury cases. It's called Colossus, and it is software designed to take an input of variables and then spit out a settlement figure. In my opinion, that end figure is only as good as the person inputting the information. I also feel that it should be used as a guideline rather than an absolute determining factor. Call me old-fashioned, but I am extremely skeptical about using computers to aid in determining values ___________ that's what people are for, after all. Common sense, wealth of experience and good sound judgment all make for an informed decision, in spite of this trend of relying on inanimate objects more and humans less.

Personally, I like the committee approach: experienced claims professionals sit down and discuss cases while getting input from other claims people about how to proceed in terms of settling. These meetings are useless, though, unless there is enough information in a file to make a good, sound decision. That's where a solid investigation into the merits of a bodily injury case really pays off. In many cases, an investigation will put the insured or insurance company in a position where, in principle, they could not offer a major settlement because of a lack of exposure or negligence. Either they defend the case or pay nuisance value money. Nuisance value money, in some instances, can be as high as $7,500. Oftentimes, a carrier will pay that kind of money to avoid litigation. Your standard insurance policy calls for paying defense costs in addition to the liability limit, and I have seen many instances where the carrier pays the policy limits and spends an additional $40,000 to $50,000 for legal fees. By paying short money, they buy peace, or an end to a claim, without having to shell out exorbitant legal expenses.

Initiation by Tire Iron

I first came upon the plague of fraud early in my career, when I worked for a large insurance firm as an independent contractor. Although working for this company gave me instant credibility, it also took advantage of my inherent talents and looked for various ways to give me work. They appreciated my excellent results. Occasionally, I would collaborate with one of their defense attorneys, and, in concert, we would uncover fraud.

Ten days before a trial was to begin, a subpoena was issued for specific medical records at Good Shepherd Hospital in Barrington, Illinois. The accident had involved an asphalt truck that had gone over the center line of a highway and had struck a vehicle head on. The other driver, in a pickup truck, was clearly injured, but we sincerely believed that his injuries were not as severe as his attorney had led us to believe: brain damage, with ongoing dizzy spells and headaches years after the accident had occurred were prevalent, he claimed. He had been seen by a whole host of doctors, including two neurologists. His attorney alleged that his ability to earn a living had been impaired.

I was not the initial investigator on the case, but I was asked to serve the subpoena for the hospital records, which I then received. I also asked the hospital records clerk if they had any other files on him for the past six years. She made a quick search, and I learned that he had been there six months after the accident. The hospital was more than obliging, and they gave me those records, too, though I had to pay a copy fee of $15.

As I sat in my car and reviewed the second set of records, I found something fascinating. From what I could gather, this man had been in a bar brawl six months after the accident with some bikers. The brutes had given his cerebral cortex a jolt with a tire iron and he'd gone to the emergency room at Good Shepherd Hospital. He'd been admitted for six days. The records revealed that he'd been hit over the head several times and had suffered a skull fracture as well.

When this information was revealed, in the midst of the trial, a conference was held in the judge's chambers. The end result was a $30,000 settlement rather than one for $550,000. The defense attorney was shrewd—he waited until the last minute to play the records card. The plaintiff's attorney had gone on and on about the severe nature of the head injury, as caused by the asphalt truck. He had gone so far as to present medical evidence before he knew we had discovered an intervening cause. If the case had gone to trial by jury, the defense counsel's closing argument would have been very powerful, making the plaintiff look like a liar and a fraud. This was avoided entirely by the settlement. The new guidelines for introducing evidence at such a late stage in the trial proceedings would preclude admission of that evidence.

For every case where the plaintiff is exposed with his knickers down, there are a hundred cases where damning evidence never comes to the forefront. Fraud runs rampant when investigators are incompetent or attorneys lack creativity or aggression. If the plaintiff had gone to a different hospital six months after the accident, we may have never known the truth.

Backdraft

In the late fall of 1984, my career was in a rut. Everything felt mundane. I was bored to distraction, and I desperately needed something juicy to combat the day- to-day doldrums. The work wasn't slow, but everything seemed to be a blur, where there was no starting point or finish line. I was considering an extended vacation.

I've always found, though, that when it's least expected, something always comes around to shake things up. This time, it was a phone call that made my ears perk up like an alert pit-bull's. The company calling, an insurance carrier, said that they suspected that their agent had backdated an application for insurance, therefore binding the driver. When an insured goes to an agent and gives the agent a check, the insurance agent who rep-resents not only the insured, but the insurance company, will bind the coverage, which means that the agent can speak for the insurance company and make a decision to accept coverage. The consideration for the coverage is the money.

Two days before the application had been received by the carrier, the insured had been involved in an accident that was his fault—one day after the application had been signed. My instructions were to take the agent's statement about the sequence of events, along with the insured driver's. In those cases, we would take two statements from the driver—one describing the facts, and the other regarding the insurance contract. Before I did either of these things, 1 had the potential insured sign a non-waiver agreement, which stipulated that the insurance company could not be held to provide coverage simply by undertaking an investigation. The insured would sign the agreement acknowledging that the carrier could investigate first, and then decide whether coverage would be in order later, depending upon what the investigation revealed.

The agreement had been signed when I met with the agent and the insured at the agent's office. At least they got their stories straight: the application was signed and a check had been delivered to the agent before the accident. The funny thing was, the application had been received by the carrier after the accident had occurred. This, of course, promoted healthy skepticism. 1 had seen this happen many times over the years, and it had ruined many a relationship between a company and an agent.

On that day, the insured's body language suggested to me that he was not telling the truth. Body language is not only manifested by a lack of eye contact, it's also a nervous twitch, or pulling on one's ears, a general sense of nervousness or unrest that is fairly easy to detect. This guy had a hard time making eye contact with me and generally was skittish. The agent was a better actor, and professed innocence in the entire matter. There was a third-party claimant that we also contacted, and we took a statement to learn more particulars of the claim. The third-party claimant was the person who had been hit by the insured. We warned this third party that coverage was not guaranteed, and that they should report the incident to their own carrier. As I looked at the papers, I couldn't help but notice that the application appeared to have been tampered with on the date line. A few days after the initial meeting, I called the insured and the agent. I wanted to see if perhaps they wanted to back off their assertion that the insurance had been arranged prior to the accident.

A couple of weeks later, I was watching the 10 o'clock news when I saw the insured on television. He was being interviewed about a surgical operation that had left his wife with brain damage. Some surgical paraphernalia had been left in her body. She had received $11 million from the hospital, and the doctor's carrier was still considering a settlement. I called the insured to express my condolences, and then I asked him whether he still wanted his carrier to address the third-party claim. He said he would settle the claim of the third party himself. The carrier was thrilled not to have to file a messy declaratory action to resolve the coverage issue. I suppose in his case, a stab at fraud was actually outshined by the powers that be.

Lug Nuts Caught on Camera

Later in my career, in the dead of winter, at 10 degrees Fahrenheit, with a 30-mile per hour wind blowing furiously from the north, I stood in a high-crime area of Chicago, waiting for a gentleman claiming to have a bad back problem, surrounded by a menagerie of howling, ferocious dogs. I was hoping not to attract any attention. This fellow, who worked for a Midas Muffler franchise, had allegedly injured his back lifting a heavy box. That's what the report said, anyway. Mr. "Jones" had been to see two doctors, an orthopedist and a chiropractor. He hadn't been seen at work for nine weeks, as he complained that he could hardly walk.

The insurance company was skeptical, so they had arranged an independent medical exam with an orthopedic doctor who, for a fee, would examine the claimant and would pass judgment as to whether the injury was legitimate or not. Mr. Jones was, of course, sent to a respected orthopedic doctor, who worked mainly for insurance carriers, though he saw his own patients as well. His fee ranged from $200 to $1,500 per visit. As a rule, this doctor did not examine patients for the plaintiff's bar, which entailed giving a completely unbiased assessment of the patient's health based on a variety of factors. First, the doctor would ask the patient about his subjective complaints; then he would test the patient for range of motion, which involved exercises like bending over and touching the toes with the doctor observing carefully. He might then order x-rays or some other means of diagnostic testing.

When the insurance carrier initially called me to see if I would take on the case, it had suggested its suspicion that Mr. Jones was either a phony or a malingerer. In industry parlance, a "malingerer" refers to a person who may in fact have been hurt, but who isn't in any hurry to return to work. I asked for some background information, including his age, a physical description, and the name of the doctor he was seeing. I also found out the date, time, and place where the exam was to take place, and I assured the insurance company that I would carefully check the fellow out.

I arrived in the man's neighborhood at 6:25 a.m. and waited in my car for a very long while. Unfortunately, I had no idea which of the many vehicles on the street belonged to him. I did know that his exam was to take place at 8:00 a.m., three miles away from his home. Finally, at 8:15, he sauntered out of his apartment building with his crutches under his right arm, positioned horizontally. I immediately noted his athletic gait. He approached a beat-up blue Torino, opened the door, and threw the crutches in the back seat. He did not seem to be in any particular hurry, even though he would clearly be over a half hour late for his appointment.

I watched as he started the car and let it run for about two minutes or so, revving the engine loudly, ostensibly to warm the car up more rapidly. My engine was already running—I was pre-pared to follow him—but as he started to pull away, he stopped abruptly. To my utter surprise, and his as well, it appeared the man's car had a flat tire. I immediately knew that this was one of those golden opportunities. I scrambled for my video camera, and with unadulterated delight, I filmed him as he deftly changed the tire. My camera and I observed that he had absolutely no difficulty crouching and lifting. He removed the lug nuts with nary a problem. I even got a close-up of his face, which showed no stress at all.

When he was just about finished, I set down my camera and opened the car door to confront him. Using some artistic license, I told him I was doing an article about the neighborhood for the local newspaper. I asked him some basic questions: "How long have you lived here? Is there a neighborly spirit on your block?" He answered my questions briefly, but without suspicion. Then I asked for his name, telling him that I would be using it in the article. I was almost positive he was my subject, but I wanted to be sure. When he happily provided me with his full name, I knew I had my man.

I went straight to my office and watched the video. It was very damning indeed. Later in the day, 1 learned that the doctor hadn't been able to find anything inherently wrong with his back. Soon after, the insurance company cut him off completely from any and all benefits. The case went to trial at the Industrial Commission, a group who adjudicates workers' compensation claims. In Illinois, and most other states, you cannot sue your employer under most circumstances. When an employee is hurt on the job, the issue doesn't end up in civil court, it is resolved by the Industrial Commission. With the video surveillance evidence I provided, the conclusion was reached that the insurance company owed Mr. Jones not a red cent.

Avarice in the City

There must be an awful lot of folks out there who think claims professionals are drooling dunces. I say so because it's usually so blatantly obvious. The public must think that claims professionals don't check, and double-check, any questionable damages presented as fact.

There is a law firm that, by design, has a philosophy: You must inflate and sculpt, and build a case from a damages standpoint. This is not only unethical, but if caught, the principals in the firm can be disbarred. Anonymously, I reported this particular firm to the Attorneys Registration Disciplinary Commission, which is a body that investigates complaints about shady and unethical dealings perpetuated by their own rank and file. In other words, it is an organization of lawyers policing other lawyers. In truth, they have a reputation for not tolerating any nonsense, and they purport to be objective. I believe they take their job seriously. Lawyers as a whole get a bad rap for committing unscrupulous deeds, including obstruction of justice, promoting perjury and bending the fabric of the law in a Machiavellian manner. P.I. attorneys and divorce attorneys share a similar low public-approval rating. Accountants aren't far behind.

Whether a particular claimant and that same law firm both conspired to defraud a self-insured company out of more than \$200,000, we will never know, but I think it was a team effort. The claimant was certainly the culprit in this case of fraud.

This is the story: Bonnie Stearns had been hit from behind, quite forcefully, on the Kennedy Expressway. Her property dam-age was more than \$12,000, which indicated the severity of the impact. Stearns had many medical complications, although they only documented soft tissue injuries. She had an MRI and CAT scans, which are expensive, but the tests showed a normal cervical spine and a normal lumbar spine. She had no herniated disks or bulges. She saw six doctors of varying specialties, complaining of severe migraine-like headaches. She also claimed that she had lost her equilibrium, but that it could not be attested to with a high degree of certainty by her doctors.

For ten months, we went back and forth with the attorney to try and pressure them to document her problems and provide us with bills and records. We made it clear that we would not consider her claim unless we're provided with an authorization form to secure an independent study of the bills and records and lost-income information. We were refused at first, but I insisted once we saw the bills and lost-time letter. 1 desperately wanted that authorization form. They were asking for $225,000, maintaining that the woman had a permanent head injury in light of her chronic and severe headaches. She was under the care of a neurologist who was charting her brainwaves.

The problem we had was that the company I represented had a high exposure because of the primary insurance limits. They had the primary coverage, and provided a self-insured exposure for bodily injury or property damage up to $500,000. The person responsible for the accident I was investigating had taken out a million dollars in coverage with the self-insured company while driving one of their rental cars.

I kept asking myself why they wanted to settle the matter now, before the statute of limitations would run out, mandating filing a lawsuit. If it was a legitimate claim, then the upside potential rendered it worth waiting. After all, the woman was still under treatment. I made a second attempt to get the authorization form; they wouldn't give us one. I perused very carefully the medical records and bills that they had sent, and I called the company that she worked for as an independent contractor, even though I did not have an authorization form to inquire about whether the information in the letter we had from them was accurate. They were alleging $65,000 in lost income.

At first, judging from the letter, I couldn't tell if she was an employee or an independent contractor, but we had been told by the attorney that she was an independent contractor. I asked for the director of human resources, and finally got this person on the phone. I explained that the attorney would not give us an authorization form, but that they could confirm the information in the letter. What piqued their interest was the large amount being claimed. Two days later, we received a call saying that she worked for them as an independent contractor, performing the services of a graphic artist. The most she had ever made in one year was $10,000, and she had no large contract or prospect of making more than $15,000 in any calendar year.

Furthermore, the letter written on her behalf had been created by someone who worked for this well-known firm, but had been let go because of attendance issues. No wonder we couldn't contact her, which was what we had tried to do initially, before contacting the human resource manager. The woman who wrote the fraudulent letter had no authority to author such a letter. With this in mind, we asked for a new letter from the company, which we received by fax, saying in rather terse language that the letter regarding the lost income of the graphic artist had been a fabrication and not authorized by the company.

The attorney was furious, and not particularly loquacious, when he heard the news. I told him, without being too specific, that their client had submitted information about her claim that was clearly fraudulent. The attorney knew exactly what I meant, but he told me he was still looking for $100,000 to settle the claim. I called the company and told them I thought we could probably settle the matter for under $50,000. The woman had $14,000 in medical bills, and they responded by giving me $45,000 in authority. I was forced to tell the attorney that we did not take this attempt to present fraudulent components of dam-ages lightly, and he disavowed any responsibility for submitting the lost-wage claim, saying that they had written a letter asking for information and the company had responded by putting it in writing. They had to take it at face value.

Even though I never specifically mentioned the lost-income issue, the attorney must have read my mind. I knew then that a serious accommodation was about to be made by the attorney to settle. Finally, the case was settled for $37,500. The impression I got was that the law firm wanted to distance itself from the mat-ter as expeditiously as possible. The woman probably did have had some medical problems from such a big hit, and she'd lost some income. She probably would have problems down the road. They'd simply let greed get the best of them and had gone over-board. Was this another victory for the good guys?

I've Got a Bridge I'll Sell Ya

In 1983, a couple in a car was hit from behind, causing $2,000 in damage to their automobile. The woman was in the front passenger seat, and hospital records showed that she had struck her face on the windshield. Seat belt laws in the state of Illinois were not yet in effect. She made a bodily injury claim for soft tissue injuries to her neck and back, and she was diagnosed with both a neck and back sprain and strain. The damage to their car was substantial enough for us to believe her claims. Appearances can be deceiving, however.

When I had the chance to interview her and her spouse, she also claimed that her dental bridge had broken as a result of the impact—the work had been done a year prior to the accident. I asked for the name of the dentist who had done the work, and she told me he had relocated to Arizona. I then requested the name of her current dentist, and 1 had her sign an authorization form so that I could communicate with him. The new dentist wrote back to me, reporting that the bridge had been broken in the accident. He said that he had disposed of the broken bridge, and had made a new one for her at a cost of $2,500. It was at that point that I contacted a national dental association, found the woman's old dentist, and I phoned him.

In a rather surprised tone, he denied ever doing any work on her bridge. He gave me the name of the dentist who had taken over his practice, and I wrote this dentist a letter. He soon called and said that he had made a bridge for her about a month prior to the accident. When she was being fitted for the device in the dental chair, he had requested that she bite down on the bridge. It had broken right then and there. He had considered making an entirely new bridge for her, but she denied him the authorization to do so. I was certainly obliged to explain to him what this woman was attempting to do in terms of her claim. She was pulling a scam on several layers, having devised an elaborate scheme to try to get her bridgework paid for, when in fact it had not ever been damaged in an auto accident. She'd enlisted the aid of a dentist who could have lost his license if we had pursued it.

Though he didn't express it freely, I could tell he was disgusted; not only was she trying to get us to pay for a bridge that had not been damaged in the accident, she was also perpetuating fraud with the aid of another dentist. I didn't waste a minute of thought on the notion that the dentist who had disposed of the bridge was unaware that the accident had been a phony, at least as far as the dental crisis.

The dentist who had fitted her for the bridge had never been paid, and that was pretty good incentive for him to cooperate with us. I informed the carrier about the facts, and I inquired whether they wanted to prosecute. After consulting with one of their defense attorneys, they decided that we could offer a reasonable settlement regarding the soft tissue injuries that she had suffered. However, if she wouldn't agree to our terms, we would be forced to consider taking legal action against her and her dentist.

I communicated our proposal to the couple. Her immediate response was, "I don't care what you say! I want $10,000 or you can leave!" I had offered her a settlement of $2,000, which was $500 above and beyond the medical bills she had incurred for her soft tissue injuries. Soft tissue injuries are bumps and bruises, short of lacerations, and do not involve fractures or permanent injuries. Keeping my cool, I directed my conversation to her husband, who had a rather pained look on his face. I "confided" in him that I felt his wife did not comprehend the gravity of the situation. I gave him two options: I could leave, or he could take his wife aside and they could discuss a plan of action. He elected the latter, and I flipped through a magazine while they deliberated.

Ten minutes later, he returned to the living room alone. "What is the most you would be willing to offer?" he asked politely. I reiterated the $2,000 offer, and we settled the case by drawing up the release forms immediately. The woman, head bowed, entered the room for as long as it took to sign her name on the dotted line and never showed her face again. The carrier was very pleased. Fraud had been exposed, and the matter had been handled without any nasty scenes.

Get Your Story Straight

Bernardo Colon, a gentleman living in a Hispanic neighbor-hood, broke his leg on Easter Sunday around 1 1:00 a.m. It was a particularly cold day, the high being around 39 degrees with snow flurries. There was nary a thought of how close spring would be, at least not yet.

There are lots of ways to break one's leg. Mr. Colon broke his by falling down from the first floor landing of his building, which led to a door just inside the front entry of his six- flat complex. It was reported that the cause of the fall was a broken step the third step down from the first floor landing, which was constructed of wood. When I went out there for a look, I saw that the tread was broken, and there was no carpet. I checked with the owner of the building, whose carrier had hired me. The insured said he had received no complaints about a broken step until after the accident, and nobody in the building claimed to know any-thing about the broken step until after Mr. Colon had suffered his accident. I found the lighting to be adequate.

Colon told a convincing story about his fall. He said that as he'd fallen, his left leg had ended up underneath the weight of his entire body. His fall had been broken, prematurely, just before he'd hit the door at the bottom of the steps. When questioned, he said he didn't know how long the step had been broken, but he said it had been covered by paper. Indeed, there were fliers scattered on the flight of stairs that obscured the broken step. Colon also told me that he had gripped the railing to his left as he'd descended. His right leg had actually made contact with the door at the bottom of the steps, retarding his momentum.

There was no maintenance man assigned to police the building on a regular basis, but one of the tenants got a break in his rent for shoveling snow and keeping the common areas clean. That tenant, judging from the looks of the building, was not carrying out his duties in an exemplary fashion. He also claimed to know nothing about the mysterious collapsed step in question until after the accident.

I knew something about the scenario simply wasn't right, so I told Mr. Colon that I needed an authorization to get his medical records, his bills and his employment records. He worked at a knife-sharpening business, making $9 an hour. Because his fracture required the insertion of hardware in his left leg, his recovery was slow. He had missed four months of work. I secured the medical records, but I was not surprised by the history given at the hospital. According to their records, Colon was disposing of a washing machine with a neighbor and a cousin. He had been at the bottom, guiding it down the steps, when the men on the top side of the washer had lost their grasp of the appliance. The washing machine tumbled, and Colon had lost his balance. The washer landed on his left lower leg.

I was a little bit miffed that he had lied to me, but I wasn't surprised—people do it all the time. I wasn't overly put out, but I decided to go back and interview him again. At first, he continued to insist that he knew nothing about any washing machine. When I asked the translator to read him the history given at the hospital, though, he miraculously changed his story and admitted the truth. I returned the favor: the insurance carrier would be sending him a letter denying his claim. He looked like his feelings were hurt, but my sympathy was running low; I told him that we didn't appreciate his fictitious story and his complete lack of candor.

The other significant factor in this case was the fact that everyone in the building had dummied up to protect him. They all knew what had really happened, including the tenant with the common area responsibility. The building was structurally sound, but not particularly clean or well-maintained. I didn't see any pronounced gouges in the walls or door demonstrating that a large rectangular object like a washing machine had fallen down the steps. We never found out how the step was damaged. In the end, the insurance company saved $75 to a $100,000 by virtue of my insistence on a thorough investigation.

Stolen Black Angus

A carrier I had worked with before hired me to conduct an investigation into a fidelity and surety claim. A meat-packing business

in Bridgeport suspected that employees were stealing inventory. The business' policy had a limit of $75,000, with a $5,000 deductible, but the insurance company had appointed a very combative lawyer. The attorney representing the insured, however, was equally fierce. On two separate occasions, I was forced to restrain them from exchanging blows, thus helping them to avoid the embarrassment of filing battery charges against each other.

The theft problem had gone on for two and a half years, and management had been extremely lax regarding security issues. I knew I was more likely to hear the truth from ex-employees than from current employees, so I tracked down several---there were differing versions in their stories.

The language in the policy mandated that the carrier was responsible for conducting an honest and fair investigation with-out attempting to look the other way if it was apparent there was a real issue about theft. Our investigation took two and a half months, including many early morning meetings with management at the south-side site. After speaking to the ex-employees, I turned my attention to several current employees. Even though management had been naive about instituting proper security measures, their policy stated that this oversight could not be held against them as a means of mitigating the dollar value of a claim.

As it turned out, management had appointed someone to handle the employee program for buying meat. I was surprised that many employees bought meat at cost, most buying cheaper cuts of meat at less than $2 a pound. The sum was then deducted from their paychecks. The trusted employee in charge of the buying system was, however, regularly doling out much better cuts of meat, valued, in some cases, at $20 a pound. Furthermore, one employee was putting meat in trash cans on the loading dock, and then transferring the meat to the trunk of his car at break time. My investigation uncovered that one industrious fellow even had his own meat stand at 47th and Cicero in Chicago, where he was selling "his" product to the public on weekends. We got the evidence on film, and he was later indicted and fired.

I kept the information to myself, and never told management, but I made a conservative guess that at least $250,000 worth of meat had been pilfered.

The two attorneys involved continued to fight bitterly, albeit verbally, while I played the role of peacemaker. It became almost comical. How they ever negotiated a settlement was beyond me, but they finally agreed on the sum of $37,000. The moral of the story? It's hard to make a profit when you can't sell what you think you own.

A Damsel in Distress?

Before 1987, I had never interviewed a woman who had been sexually assaulted. I don't believe anyone who hasn't been through such a horrifying experience can begin to understand the angst brought about by such a vile act. I read case studies of rape victims, and I noted with interest that there seemed to be a certain pattern affecting rape victims which included a period of time, varying in length, where the victim fell into an introverted, introspective cocoon full of colossal hurt and utter revulsion. I learned that it was also common for the victim to grapple with unabashed feelings of self-loathing. With this knowledge, it seemed to me to go against human nature, particularly female human nature, for the victim of this heinous crime to become boastful about the "killing" she would make when she settled the case with her insurance company. When I heard this woman say exactly that, I was surprised, to say the least.

The woman's chief complaint was that the apartment complex where she lived had what she referred to as "inadequate" locks on the windows. She lived in an English-style basement apartment, and the window that had been used to gain access to her apartment was low enough so as not to necessitate any climbing on the part of the perpetrator —a monster indeed—to get in. The building was more than 20 years old, and the windows and locks had apparently been in the process of being changed when the alleged rape had taken place. According to the police, the victim had been hysterical upon their arrival, and there appeared to be signs of forced entry on her bedroom window. The window was broken; as was the lock, which may have been broken for some time prior to the alleged attack. The woman described the rapist as wearing a nylon stocking over his face, and the police could not find any fingerprint samples definitive enough to make identification. The victim also attended three suspect line-ups, and was shown several photos of possible rapists. She made no positive ID. An ex-boyfriend was tracked down, and after thorough questioning, was deemed not to be a suspect.

This "victim's" plan was to sue the building complex and its managing agent while eventually moving out. But a year and a half later, she was purported to be bragging in a suburban bar about the brand-new conversion van she was going to buy with the tax-free windfall she was anticipating as a result of the suit. Unfortunately for her, the building manager caught wind of these comments. I am fully aware that the world is a very small place. You never know who's talking to whom.

After I was contacted, I urged the insurance company to hire a surveillance expert with a concealed camera and microphone to capture her on film and audio when she was in one of those "bare your soul" moods. We identified the bar she frequented and sent three different people in there to chat her up. Sure enough, one Friday night, when she was sotted, she related her story of avarice to our plant. She never admitted to not being raped, but her consistent revelations, to strangers even, concerning the money, money, money made a few of us very skeptical.

Despite this very relevant information, the insurance carrier was afraid to take the case to court. They compromised and settled for $50,000, which was much less than the woman thought she'd receive. Her own lawyers expressed their doubts, though subtly—the deal was a compromise.

At one point, we had a female psychiatrist consult with us regarding the situation. She felt, after hearing the woman's revelations, that she was most probably disingenuous about the whole affair. Certainly I'll never know what happened. Rape is such a serious matter, you'd think it would be off limits when it comes to fraudulent attempts to make money. Everyone reacts differently after a personal tragedy, but this person did not behave like a victim __________ she behaved like an opportunist. Could it be that a lover had crawled in through her window and had sparked an idea? I've found that there is nothing too sacred to sacrifice if greed is the main motivation.

A Hole in the Head

I investigate every case as if it has the potential to go to trial. The truth is, most don't. It's the cost factortrials involve attorneys and expert testimony fees and there are other miscellaneous expenses.

A statement given is evidence, and sometimes statements can be used to impeach a witness, or even a claimant. In some instances, medical records can be very valuable in revealing what really happened in an accident. Hospitals require information about the injury and it is entered into the patient's medical records. In many instances, the history given refutes the purported account of how a person came to be injured.

A woman on a golf course claimed to have been struck in the head while standing by the cart return area. She theorized that the course was liable because the cart return area was too close to the ninth hole and thus unsafe. The golf course owners (the insured) were very uncooperative and made it difficult for me to talk to their employees. A suit was eventually filed, and after several months, I was still being stymied by a lack of cooperation. The president of the corporation who owned the golf course hid under the auspices of his supercilious personal attorney.

My suggestion to the carrier was to threaten to deny coverage if they didn't step up. I wrote my idea about this to the personal attorney, and he called the claims manager at the carrier and demanded that I be removed from the case. The insurance company agreed I was summarily dismissed because of my criticism regarding the corporate attorney's tactics in representing the interests of the golf course.

Before my bill was paid, though, I learned something very interesting. Apparently, the injured woman's medical records stated, verbatim: *"patient states she fell out of a moving golf cart and hit her head "* Even more alarming and gleeful (for me) was that the records said her blood work showed she was clearly intoxicated, at a .25!

Just When You Thought You'd Heard it All

The most memorable case I investigated involving fraud and alcohol was the story of a fellow who checked into a motel with his wife on a Friday afternoon around 3 o'clock p.m. When he checked in, the clerk remembered him saying, "Bring on the dancing girls!" He had been slurring his words and gave every indication of being soused. Later that afternoon, he fell in the bathtub, broke his hip, and suffered a skull fracture. The bathtub had a nonskid surface. The man argued that he'd had nothing to grab onto as he'd fallen. I pressured his attorney so much, he withdrew from the case. He knew he was skating uphill.

When I finally interviewed this guy and his wife, the truth came out. He admitted consuming seven beers and two shots of Jack Daniels prior to falling. He had started drinking around 12:30 p.m. that day. He and his wife were on their way to a Christmas party near the motel and he was getting a jovial early start. The hospital records revealed his blood alcohol to be 0.26. The case was denied. Some folks, I believe, are simply too foolish to succeed at fraud.

Ignorance Personified

I interviewed a claimant in his attorney's office in Glen Ellyn, which is in DuPage County. Within five minutes, I realized this particular claimant would never make it in front of a jury. He was incredibly annoying and wouldn't shut up. His attorney told him at least 50 times, "Just answer the question!" He had an uncanny propensity for misusing vocabulary, and possessed the antithesis of the art of verbal acuity. My favorite malapropism was when he said, in reference to his job, "I was orientated to do the work disputably."

I learned in the interview that the man's vehicle had been impacted __ hard from behind, while he'd been at a stoplight. Liability was not in question. It was all about damages, and he had an acute back problem that could probably be related to the accident. He'd even had surgery. In looking at his medical records, I believed it was legitimate. The attorney gave me a package of bills and records to send to the carrier, and I also quizzed the guy, trying to get a word in edgewise, about lost income. He hadn't worked since the accident. I found it interesting that at age 31 he was still living with his mother. I also found out that he had never filed taxes. He was an independent contractor for a meat wholesaler; he sold meat door to door. The most he'd ever made in any given year was $15 to $20,000. To him, that didn't merit filing taxes.

I called the company and told them what I'd found out. I told the defense attorney that the jury would despise his client. He had two major problems: he was a big mouth, and he was in hot water with the IRS. The carrier offered

$55,000 to settle, and his attorney rejected the offer. They were looking for 100,000 bucks or more. The carrier was kind enough to extend the offer for a month, and the man's attorney said he would produce his client in person, hoping that after seeing him, the carrier would be more favorably disposed to settling the case. Instead, the opposite effect took place. Someone anonymously tipped off the IRS, and the guy was audited. The case went to trial, and the jury, after hearing the defense counsel's arguments and the impassioned pleas from the plaintiff's attorney to treat his client fairly, came back with an award of one dollar! I was lucky enough to see it myself.

CHAPTER 4: CHILDHOOD CRISES AND CRIMES

The public should be aware that signing a release of all claims and taking consideration (a check) in exchange for giving the insurance company that release is almost as absolute, as we say in America, as "death and taxes." I always tell people before they sign: Once you take the money, you are history. In other words, you have no recourse to come back at a later date and ask for additional money.

A parent/guardian release can be broken if it can be shown that whatever ailments a child has currently is related to some type of accident or occurrence where a tort (committing a wrong against another person) was committed. Committing a tort doesn't necessarily mean hitting someone over the head; a tort is basically a negligent action causing physical harm or property damage. It can be leaving a roller skate on your front steps, or a hose across your sidewalk. Hitting another person or vehicle with your car can be considered a tort. It can be a breach of duty to a guest or a person coming into your home or business if there is a hazard, or something is awry which results in an accident involving bodily injury.

A parent/guardian release is signed by a parent, or parents, when they are making a judgment call by taking money from the insurance company to settle the child's claim. The child, of course, cannot enter into a contract until the age of 18. There is language in the parent/guardian release stating that the party who breaks the release agrees to pay back the insured for any additional money that may be spent to settle the claim. It is rather curious language, which seems to suggest that the party breaking the release better have a compelling reason to do so. In 27 years, I have never seen a release of this type broken or, for that matter, never have I seen an attempt to do so.

The most difficult cases I've worked on have involved children. There is nothing more tragic than a child who suffers an injury, or loses his/her life, because responsible parties aren't on the ball; watching kids as kids must be watched.

Leap Frog

In DuPage County, there are very few high-rise buildings. In Lisle, there are a couple of 10- story buildings, side by side, housing mostly lower-income people. When I went to see one of these building owners, I found him to be an interesting fellow and very cooperative as well. The reason for my visit was that one of his tenants' children had climbed out onto a ledge, had broken through a screen, and had dropped 60 feet to the ground below. The 4-year-old boy had mercifully landed on the grass and had survived, but he was severely injured with fractured bones and a damaged spleen that had to be removed. The building in question had built-in ledges that were three feet high ___ any child could conceivably climb up on them and gain access to the windows.

On the day of the incident, it had been very warm, the window had been open, and the child had been pushing on the screen when it gave way. His mother had been in the bathroom talking on the phone at the time her child had fallen.

Because humans have such a strong tendency to fix blame wherever they possibly can, the mother promptly sued the building owner for the improper design of the windows. It was too late to bring in the architect and the construction company; the building was well over 15 years old. The lawsuit alleged that the three-foot high ledges, wide enough to crawl on, and level with the bottom of the windows, were inherently dangerous. In the state of Illinois, case law states that screens are not constructed to restrain humans or animals.

I nosed around the building and conversed with several ten-ants, including five adults and one teenager. Everyone knew about the child's fall, and all of them said the same thing: the mother was negligent because she was not watching her child. One woman went so far as to admit to the police that she'd seen the child climbing on the ledge numerous times, out of sight of his mother. The police report affirmed that the mother had been on the phone, away from her toddler, for well over five minutes. The most flabbergasting piece of information I picked up, though, was that another child, a 3-year-old boy, had fallen out of a window on the seventh floor where his mother had removed the screen herself, seven months after the first incident had occurred. The window had been wide open to let the warm spring breeze in. The two units even shared the identical ledge! In the second case, the child had figured out how to climb up on the ledge beneath a wall of windows, and out he'd gone. This poor kid had fallen 70 feet and had landed in the bushes.

Remarkably, he suffered only a couple of minor scratches.

I remember reading once that during a tornado, a straw had blown clear through a thick tree trunk. I recall thinking it was like something out of *Ripley's Believe It or Not*. The fact that these two children had survived the ignorance of their parents and a huge fall belongs in the record books, too. Though I wasn't privy to the details of the outcome of this case, it's my guess that the carrier made a compromised settlement at some point despite the case law mentioned above. It is my sincere hope that the parents of these boys realize both their blessings and their mistakes.

Heavy Metal is Dangerous

Many older buildings—the city of Chicago is rife with them--have been painted both on the exterior and interior with lead-based paint. What many people don't know is that even if you paint over the original, potentially dangerous paint several times, the lead permeates through. Most, if not all, small children and babies, like to put objects in their mouth. In a syndrome known as "pica," some children have a craving for unnatural food. In most instances, "pica" is caused by malnutrition. In this case, what children may have been putting in their mouths was very dangerous.

The city of Chicago has a lead poisoning unit, which is part of the Department of Health. Like most important bureaucracies, they don't have suitable computers, and their records are in complete disarray. I know this because I've been there many times perusing their records, which have been moved three times in 20 years. The lead poisoning unit will allow anyone to inspect their files, but nothing can be removed from the premises or copied. Personally, I've used a recording device to help me remember the contents of what I've seen, or I can always take copious notes. Sadly, Department of Health agents are asked to perform their jobs using unsophisticated instruments of highly questionable accuracy to quantify the amount of lead in paint chips, which are measured by parts per million. The parts per million standard should not exceed federal government guidelines, or it is considered dangerous.

The result is unfortunate: in many low-income neighbor-hoods, conditions that foster lead poisoning in children are all too prevalent. In fact, the Center for Disease Control has a myriad of statistics regarding lead poisoning in children. Inattentive parents or guardians and landlords perpetuate the problem ____

they even encourage it sometimes to save money. I am often amazed by the squalor people surround themselves with. Even the poverty-stricken can choose cleanliness.

The main culprit in lead poisoning is the ingestion of paint chips. There are other factors, which may come in the form of dust, contaminated water, or good old-fashioned contaminated dirt. An adult can absorb much more lead than a child and not be harmed, although over long periods of exposure, brain damage is common. In children, this is manifested by a reduced ability to learn, listlessness, irritability and sleeplessness. Drugs have been developed to combat this problem, but those with very high levels of lead in the bloodstream are often beyond constructive help.

In my line of work, the questions of whether brain damage has occurred, and how to quantify it, are the most common. In low-income neighborhoods there are complexities in the matter of measuring the potential to learn. Expectations are not as high as in other more prosperous neighborhoods. While it is always defeatist to subscribe to hopelessness, I must admit that I have never encountered a lead poisoning case in a high-income, or even middle-income, neighborhood. In truth, every case I have investigated has involved a HUD property or a low-income apartment building or complex.

This sad state of affairs could be solved by increased responsibility on the part of landlords, who must inspect their buildings more frequently, including individual apartments. However, most lease agreements stipulate the landlord or their representative worker (maintenance person) can not enter the demise premises (the apartment) without permission of the tenant. Typically, when a family moves into an apartment, it is painted in a standard white, indoor latex paint. When damage occurs, including holes in walls and ceilings, it needs to be patched right away with spackle and paint. Tenants can do this cheaply, using the correct methods to spare their young ones from harm, but they are often unaware of their options. There ought to be a concentrated effort to educate people about the dangers of lead paint in order to save present and future generations, and to eradicate this problem.

One of the most disturbing cases I participated in involved a little girl between the ages of 1 and 3 who had contracted unusually high levels of lead in her bloodstream, probably as a result of Pica. Over a period of months, she had become sick and listless, and doctors had been using chelating drugs— anticoagulants that help remove harmful substances from the blood, such as lead—to try to nurse her back to health. It was probable that she had *suffered* brain damage, and she was really struggling in school as she got older.

I began my investigation by first checking with the Department of Health. Both the insured and the property owner had demonstrated excellent records regarding who had painted the unit. They even had a photograph showing what the apartment had looked like before occupancy. I recognized that this insured was a step ahead of any other insured I had ever worked with. In addition to photos, he also had a lease addendum signed by the tenant acknowledging that the apartment was in tiptop condition before she'd moved in.

After the child became ill and was tested, lead had been found in the apartment's paint, but upon examination of the records, no "flaking" paint had been found except for on the exterior window sills, and in a small area in a bedroom closet. My next step was to try and get permission to talk with one of the inspectors, but the Department of Health would not allow this without a subpoena. The family's attorney produced the girl's mother to make a statement. The woman, who was unmarried with three children, had had a series of boyfriends living with her and the children off and on over the past years. Either the attorney was plain ignorant, or he knew that if we didn't pay, someone else would. Upon further investigation, I found out that the infected child had spent sever-al months with her grandparents in the last couple of years, so I checked with the city of Chicago lead poisoning unit. They had no records pertaining to the grandparents' building, which they in fact owned. The building was old, and it wasn't in particularly good condition, either inside or outside.

I knew I had to convince the lead poisoning unit to inspect the premises. At first, they refused, so I called the office of the attorneys who represented the city of Chicago and raised hell by threatening to go to the print media. Finally, the city agreed to send inspectors to the building. It turned out to be in far worse condition than the building belonging to the insured! In light of this information, we were able to involve the grandparents' carrier. By tender, we tried to get them to take the matter over and assume responsibility, but they refused. In the end, we paid $72,000 to settle the claim, and the grandparents' carrier paid 70 percent after two years of wrangling. A suit was never filed, partly because the attorney who was representing the children was in no hurry—the statute of limitations would not expire until the child's 20th birthday.

A little ingenuity goes a long way ___ the case was settled for $72,000, having been probated because it involved a minor. The court approved the settlement, the bills were paid, and an annuity was set up and purchased by the insurance company for the child's future education and living expenses so that her mother would be prevented from spending the money at her whim. In fact, she had to petition the court for any use of the funds. We had no real reason to suspect her, but unscrupulous parents and guardians are more common than one might expect.

I Just Looked Away for a Minute!

Marshall Field's was the preeminent place to shop in the Chicago area for decades. The name Marshall Field's was synonymous with quality merchandise. It still is a fine place to shop, but the competition is keener than ever now with Nordstrom's and Bloomingdale's sharing the retail arena. Sears was always the place to buy appliances, tires, batteries, or tools, and I never thought of it as a place to buy clothes, but a lot of people do. There is certainly nothing wrong with that—they have very good and competitively priced merchandise. I had a neighbor who was an executive at Sears Roebuck and Company, and he and his family always looked well dressed. They bought most, if not all of their clothes at Sears, and they looked as well-groomed as anyone when the occasion called for it. I saw his wife once at Target. It must have been an emergency run for something desperately needed.

In the 70s and 80s, the retail climate was really starting to change with the entrance of the K-Marts and the Wal-Marts and Target stores. Locally, the Wiebolts and Goldblatts were not doing so well with all of these new entries into the retail marketplace. Then there was Montgomery Wards and their "electric avenue" appliance departments. None of these traditional companies are in business any longer. They all went belly up.

Before that point, however, I had a case at a Goldblatt's at 47th and Ashland. This store was in an area of the city that would be best characterized as mixed and lower-middle class. By and large, it is predominantly Hispanic. This store was also in the heart of the "back of the yards" area, where until just after WWII, cattle were slaughtered. Thinking back, I miss the Damen Overpass (just west of the "back of the yards" area), which allowed one to travel over a mile without stopping—something almost unheard of in the city of Chicago. Furthermore, it boasted a panoramic view; you could even see the downtown skyline on a clear day because of its elevation. The Damen Overpass was closed when I last passed that way.

The Goldblatt's store had a potpourri of jewelry and cosmetics on the first floor, and a grand stairway led to the second floor, which housed the clothing department. One day, a mother, Maria Estevez, came into the store with her two boys—one 4 years of age and the other 6. Our investigation revealed that she left the boys unattended for at least five to ten minutes. One of the clerks saw the younger boy climbing on the railing at the second floor level—it was 17 feet to the floor below. The clerk who saw this warned the boy, but the boy didn't speak English, only Spanish. The clerk should have called security and physically gone over to where the boy was, gently removed him from the railing, and led him to find his mother, but she didn't. Security apparently had monitors in a back room so they could watch all areas of the store; frequently, they would make announcements over the intercom to remind parents to keep an eye on their children. It was a real problem at this particular store, which I learned while conversing with the security staff, and later with salespeople who gave testimony regarding what became a terrible accident.

The little boy was not deterred by anyone. His mother was nowhere in sight, and the kid fell to the terrazzo floor below. It took the store personnel five to seven minutes to find the mother. The boy was badly injured, suffering a skull fracture and several internal injuries. As a result, he had his spleen removed. The mother spoke broken English and excellent Spanish. I talked to her before she hired an attorney, but she wouldn't tell me anything about his injuries, nor would she tell me about the accident. Maybe she had an attorney all along and simply didn't tell me right away. That happens frequently. The problem with this case was that the clerk could potentially have stopped the accident from occurring, but she was too absorbed in her work to take action. The mother was also culpable—more so than the store— because it was her job and responsibility to keep watch over her own children.

The boy recovered, but I don't know how well. The insurance carrier was afraid of the case, as well they should have been, in spite of the mother's flat out negligence. The law says that you cannot impute any negligence to a 4-year-old, so eventually the case was settled for $95,000—factored into the settlement amount was the mother's negligence. It could have been a lot worse. The mother eventually found a fairly high-profile attorney, but not directly. She was referred by a local neighborhood lawyer who had never seen the inside of a courtroom.

The fact was, the railing was sturdy, more than three and a half feet in height, and well within Building Officials and Code Administration (BOCA) code, which the city of Chicago uses. It could be argued that the store should not have been forced to anticipate this type of horseplay, and this may be a correct assumption. Numerous appellate court case decisions maintain that an open and obvious risk, as it pertains to heights, warrant a finding of no liability or no duty to the owner of the property. Furthermore, the courts consistently hold that a parent is responsible for a child's welfare.

Even though a careful study of case law would suggest that it was an eminently defensible case, the insurance carrier was still leery. This was owed primarily to the uncertainty of what a Cook County jury would do regarding a case with so many cross cur-rents. It would be particularly difficult to overlook the child's tender age. With no possibility of imputing negligence to the child because of his age, the focus would then center on the negligence attributed to the store. One of the main issues in the case was whether the owner of the store had done anything wrong.

There was a case in Illinois where the appellate court had held that a storeowner had no duty to 4-year-old that had fallen. The reasoning was, even a 4-year-old should have appreciated the danger, as it was obvious. There was much hand wringing involved. Would we settle or defend? The law on cases that had been decided before provided a barometer for viewing a similar set of facts. However, there was no exact formula. Facts are not always the same, and juries don't always come to the same conclusions. There was a lot of second-guessing and tough decisions to make.

This case illustrates why carriers settle rather than risk a larger dent in the pocketbook, even though it might appear to be a case that can be defended successfully, resulting in a not-guilty verdict or a summary judgment. A summary judgment occurs when a judge feels that there is not enough evidence of wrongdoing to continue on with the case. He or she dismisses the case before it ever goes to trial.

Escalator Escapades

My older brother and I were fooling around in a store at the Evergreen Plaza called Litton's. I was a small tyke, about 8 years old, and my brother was 11. We may have been at the shopping center on our own since we only lived four short blocks away.

Litton's had an escalator that connected the two levels of the store, and as we were going up the escalator, my brother didn't pick up his feet as the steps flattened out and traveled underneath the grate. He had a brand-new pair of P.F. Flyers, a primarily black high-top gym shoe with a white rubber sole and white rubber around the toe. He was damned proud of those shoes! The escalator chopped off the right front part of his shoe, but fortunately it didn't take his toes along for the ride. I-low he extricated himself was a miracle. His reflexes must have been quick, because he yanked his right foot away at the last possible second. The escalator didn't even stop. He was very lucky.

I vaguely remember encountering an employee in the store, but I don't believe a formal report was made. In the late 1950s, the public was not nearly as claims-conscious as they are today. Business establishments hack then weren't as paranoid about their exposure to the public from a claims or liability perspective. I remember leaving the store without a lot of fanfare. I also recall feeling sorry for my brother, not because he'd almost had his toes ripped off, but because his snazzy gym shoes were ruined. I didn't have a pair myself, so I'd been slightly jealous. The envy dissipated quickly.

Escalators are fun to play on. You might characterize them as an "attractive nuisance" for a child. Some adults even like to trifle with them—the great thrill of running down the up escalator, virtually defying gravity, or running up the down escalator, which is equally tantalizing. Usually, store security frowns upon such maneuvers, obviously.

A famous furniture store in Chicago had extremely elongated escalators leading from the front entrance of the store to a mezzanine level. The escalators traveled about 150 feet. Beyond the mezzanine area was the main showroom. One day, a woman and her husband, along with their baby and stroller, were leaving the store. The down escalator had a grate at the bottom where the steps disappeared and rotated. In this instance, there were a couple of missing teeth in the grate.

The escalator was serviced by a major repair service who should have alerted the furniture store about the teeth, but they'd never made any recommendations about anything needing a replacement. The escalator was serviced regularly and was considered to be in good running order.

According to all accounts, the escalator had not malfunctioned. There was, however, no formal service contract.

The female customer happened to be an anesthesiologist, not long out of medical school. I would characterize her as being very bright. Her husband was also quite bright, and worked for a well-known law firm. They consented to meet with me, and I took statements from both of them, individually. Shortly there-after, the woman hired an attorney who asked for $300,000 to settle the case.

The story, as I saw it, went like this: The doctor had been distracted in an effort to lift the stroller, and she'd caught her right foot in the grate at the bottom of the escalator. She had been wearing sandals, and had lost part of her second toe on the right foot, along with the tip of another toe. Fortunately, the big toe on the right foot was spared. She was rushed to the hospital and had surgery to reattach the missing digit. It was a painful and harrowing experience for her, but as a doctor, she hadn't panicked. She tolerated the ordeal far better than the average person, probably. I didn't sense any great emotional scars brought on by the accident.

Her husband told me that as a 10-year-old, he had experienced an encounter with an escalator too. As a result, he'd learned where the standard shut-off switch is near the bottom of the escalator. He'd been in front of his wife, and was helping her lift the stroller when the accident occurred. He'd negotiated the bottom of the escalator just fine while lifting up the stroller. When he saw what had happened, he'd activated the switch almost immediately. He was quite shocked by what happened. His wife was only carrying a shoulder bag, so her arms and hands were free to deal with the stroller.

The injured woman related that she knew she was close to the bottom area where the escalator flattens out. She offered no cogent explanation as to why she'd gotten her foot caught. The last question I asked her was, "Did you see the warning at the top of the down escalator that states that when one gets off the escalator, one must pick up their feet?"

Her response was, "I have ridden on a thousand escalators, so I didn't need to read the warning signs." The warning signs also indicated that strollers should not be carried on the escalator. The building in question had an elevator to transport those with strollers.

Anyone knows that this particular admission wasn't exactly helpful in proving her case. I thought it was ironic that a person with her gift of intellect could be so lacking in common sense. Her first error in judgment caused her to have the accident, and her second error was to make such a startling admission that she knew all about the warnings, and the impact of not heeding the warnings! Yet she had still had the accident. I thought about what she'd look like on the stand, with the jury paying attention to her every word, as a Raymond Burr-like attorney posed some hard questions: "You mean to say in response to whether you read the warnings at the top of the escalator that you didn't need to read them because you had ridden on an escalator a thousand times? Is that what you said? Is that true?"

I imagined her flustered and unable to speak. Maybe she would look down for a long minute and ask for the question to be repeated. Her ultimate answer would have to be: "I cannot deny that"

"Raymond Burr" would give a long look at the jury, and then roll his eyes. He would bellow, "The defense rests!"

After a brief pause, the judge would say, "The case is dismissed."

In reality, the case was settled. The law firm representing her put up a lot of false bravado, at first, about why this was such a good case from a plaintiff's point of view. They had one key fact in their favor: there were missing teeth at the grate at the bottom of the escalator. They knew they would have a very difficult job in overcoming their client's stupidity, though. Surely they knew after evaluating their client that she would not garner a lot of sympathy in front of a jury. Her livelihood had not been permanently affected in any demonstrative manner. She could even have become the object of derision by jury members, given the fact that it could be shown that there were no other accidents at that particular escalator in the last 20 years. Also, the common person who has never been dumb enough to get their foot caught in an escalator might wonder how someone as smart, good-looking, and upper-class could have this happen to them. Most of her medical care had been performed gratis because she was a doctor.

The case settled for $20,000. The escalator repair company contributed $5,000 towards the settlement without involving their carrier. Maybe taking the elevator would have been a better idea.

Bang Bang

I am not a staunch advocate of keeping guns at home, whether they're locked up or not. Handguns, especially, end up in the hands of people with some strange and evil notions. The fact that violence is glorified on TV and in the movies certainly doesn't help; every other day a news report tells us about another dead child, shot needlessly. On a farm or ranch, there may be a need for a rifle or shotgun, but to me, handguns seem good for nothing. Adults must be meticulous when it comes to the way guns are stored, and kids must be warned that a loaded gun is to be given a very wide berth. Children and teenagers, especially boys, have a potent fascination with guns, yet so many lives have been ruined by these instruments of death.

I knew a couple of guys growing up who almost became part of a catastrophe. One boy's parents were out of town and a group of buddies came by to hang out. One of them was playing around with a rifle, pointing it to another boy. The kid didn't know a thing about guns and didn't realize it was loaded _________ he ended up shooting his friend in the thigh. He never lived it down, and was given the alias" Quick Draw" from then on. The injured fellow recovered, but the shooter's family moved away to avoid the constant reminders of what had transpired.

As an insurance investigator, I've taken jobs that have proven to be distasteful, but also scintillating in an odd way. Background information doesn't always explain why a tragedy occurs, and chronological events leading up to the tragic act are not always logical. Psychology and personalities often prove to be nothing short of wondrous.

I was assigned a case where a 16-year-old had shot his 15-year-old friend in his bedroom with a rifle. All of the chambers were empty except for one. The young man who was shot died six hours later. He only lived that long because the doctors made a Herculean effort to save him. He'd been shot in his left chest and a piece of the bullet had caught part of his heart.

When questioned, the shooter said he'd been playing a game of "who would blink first," or in good old American parlance, a game of chicken. It was Russian Roulette, basically. The boy's parents had been home at the time. His father owned two rifles and two handguns, which were supposed to be locked up in a crawlspace, though the father had even taught his son to shoot a rifle and handgun by the time he was 11 years old. The guns hadn't been used in six months, and Dad was unaware that his son had broken the combination lock and then bought a similar-looking lock to fool his father. The man admitted that he never checked to see if his guns had been tampered with. He'd tried to teach his son about the grave responsibilities that go with handling firearms, but the boy's fascination had been far more powerful.

The police had a field day, and privacy was definitely a secondary issue. The state ordered testing and counseling for the shooter. The dead boy's parents could have used therapy themselves __ they were in utter anguish and were very conflicted about their son. He had been going through a very troubled adolescent period and was attending a special needs school.

The question I was hired to answer was whether the shooting was intentional or not. The police were doubtful, and the shooter denied it vigorously. But I wasn't so sure. I knew that the dead boy had experienced grave emotional problems of his own, and it occurred to me that the shooter had, as a "service," bumped off his troubled friend. The shooter's family was cooperative but distant. Their pain should have been more evident or palpable, but it wasn't. Perhaps they were simply numbed by the entire experience, first with the police, then the funeral, then the repercussions. But never once did 1 see any of them cry.

The carrier who handled the matter sent a reservation of rights to the insured, the shooter's parents, stating that there may not be coverage if the investigation revealed that the shooting was an intentional act. There would never be coverage provided by a liability policy for an intentional act, but a lawsuit alleging all sorts of malicious deeds could be filed, including negligence. If anything, this would oblige the carrier to defend the insured on the negligence count, which would start to run up the legal bills.

The carrier usually controls legal bills to some degree by choosing a lawyer they know, whose fees they are comfortable with. Often, the carrier will even make a settlement for nuisance value even if they don't owe, just to limit or avoid legal costs. Lawyers know that, so they often take cases with no liability and end up making a few bucks. There are two ways the carrier pays out money for claims: they pay the claim itself, or they pay legal expenses, which include an independent adjuster expense. That's where I come in. Either choice affects the bottom line equally.

In this particularly sad and gruesome case, after receiving my reports and advice, the carrier decided that they had no recourse but to pay the $100,000 policy limit. The family who had lost a son had never hired an attorney until they heard the carrier's offer. Then, their newly found attorney realized that without a protracted legal battle, there was no way he could collect more than $100,000 for the aggrieved family. It would have meant trying to secure assets from the insured, and possibly forcing them to sell their house and possessions to meet any judgment rendered by the court. The attorney was paid $20,000, which is less than the customary one-third fee. What added to the tragedy was that we would have paid them $100,000 without the attorney. The family didn't want to drag the matter out forever, though, wisely realizing that protracted legal action can be painful emotionally for every-one involved. No amount of money would salve those hideous wounds, and the shooter's family was not wealthy by any means.

Their son, notwithstanding the scourge of what he'd caused, still faced criminal proceedings. Even though the police believed the shooting was unintentional, they weren't prepared to let him walk away with a slap on the hand. The death certificate stated that the shooting had been accidental, and the psychiatrist hired by the state opined that the boy did not possess the makeup to be abnormally violent. Upon rigorous examination and reflection, the authorities agreed that it had been an accident. Still, the state's attorney would not drop the case. After wasting an inordinate amount of the taxpayers' money, they dropped charges of involuntary manslaughter in exchange for an agreement that the boy would participate in extensive counseling until he turned 18.

A Boy and a Gun

We have all heard the phrase "the lunatics are running the asylum." I had some personal experience with this type of scenario when I dealt with a family with some troubles. I have never had a perpetually soused father-in-law, but if I did, and if I were responsible for his care, one of the first things I would do would be to take away his service revolver.

An extremely wealthy financial guru in the investment banking field owned a piece of prime property in North Barrington. The land boasted a magnificent $4. 5 million-dollar home that shared space with a smaller home worth perhaps $750,000. This rich gent's father-in-law needed constant attention, so he and his wife moved him into the smaller of the property's two homes. In exchange for room and board, the son of the couple's longtime friends moved in as well to keep an eye on Grandpa.

The 21-year old boy caretaker had made it through high school, though he had long ago become estranged from his father, and had a pile of pent-up malevolent emotions. In college, he'd begun to feel more and more like he didn't fit in. He took advantage of the free counseling that some universities provide, but he soon dropped out and returned home, where he continued to see a psychiatrist. Eventually, he was diagnosed as being bipolar (alternating periods of mania and mental depression). For his manic-depressive illness, he was put on medication for which he had to be constantly monitored, and the medication needed to be tweaked often. Like many people suffering from these diseases, he was often in a state of denial. The family, hoping to help him somehow, hired him anyway.

When Grandpa relocated from his condo to his new home, the boy helped him move and quickly discovered a cache of ammunition and a service revolver __ a Colt .45 handgun. As time passed, the boy kept silent about his discovery, though he grew fixated with the weapon. At one point, he tried to shoot a squirrel in the backyard. The property owner was not home at the time, but his own son was, and he instructed the young man to put the gun away. Not a word was mentioned about the incident, and the couple and their son apparently found nothing unusual about the boy's demeanor. Grandpa was clearly too far gone to make a proper judgment. In essence, no one was perceptive enough to fathom the potential danger.

Two days after attempting to shoot the squirrel in the back-yard, the young man took the gun downtown to meet a friend. Over the course of the day, they drank and smoked marijuana, which probably exacerbated his heightened sense of paranoia. Quite out of the blue, he pulled the gun from his pocket and accosted his friend in his apartment. He began by shoving the barrel of the gun under his friend's chin, causing the friend to, quite literally, shit in his pants while begging for his life. Something he said must have worked, because his life was indeed spared. The friend crawled out of a window and left without alerting the police or building management. Shortly thereafter, the shooter went to the lobby of the building and severely pistol whipped a fellow who was waiting for an elevator with his girl-friend. He wasn't done yet, though. Next, he broke down an apartment door and shot a Ugandan man dead. He tried to shoot the man's brother, too, but the handgun jammed. Then he left the building, waving the gun, and shouted, "I did it! I did it!" just as the police arrived en masse.

The family generously hired a top-notch criminal attorney who prepared a sagacious defense. The murderous young man was proven not guilty by reason of insanity in a bench trial, which the attorney had opted for rather than a trial by jury. A judge was far less likely to misinterpret the law or misunderstand the merits of the case in the attorney's mind. The shooter was sentenced to a high-security hospital, and is likely doped up to the hilt, with no chance of getting out, at least not any time soon. In the meanwhile, the taxpayers bear the expense of this deranged, misguided young man with easy access to a gun.

Suit was filed by the estate of the Ugandan man whose life had ended so abruptly and so inexplicably. The fellow who was pistol-whipped sought pecuniary satisfaction via the courts. There were multiple defendants with collective liability limits well beyond seven zeros. The man who had generously taken in his father-in-law, along with the disturbed caretaker, had some-how remained unaware of an unprotected deadly weapon on his property; became a defendant, along with his father-in-law. The man's son and the shooter's friend (who had been attacked him-self) were also sued. The shooter's psychiatrist was sued over not alerting the authorities of the danger presented by the troubled young man. The building was sued for lax security provisions. It all added up to a calamity of major proportions, with more ruined lives, accompanied by unmitigated pain and misery. The moral of the story is simple: if you must have one, keep your gun locked and know where it is at all times.

Unrestrained Exuberance

As a kid, I used to go to a movie house called the Avalon Theatre on the southeast side of Chicago. It had been built in the 1920s, and was a real throw-back to the great old movie palaces with an elegant main floor and a large balcony. The decor was ornate and, frankly, breathtaking. The first movie I remember seeing there was *The Ten Commandments*, at age 6.

There was a restaurant called the Kick-a-Poo Inn not more than a hundred feet away from the theater. I don't believe they were serving seven-course meals there _ the place was just a step above fast food, but it didn't claim to be a gourmet establishment. It must have been all right, because I vaguely remember eating there with my family, and my mother was somewhat fussy about where she ate. For all I know, it was our first and last visit; I simply don't recall. The Avalon Theatre is still there today, but the restaurant met its demise and was torn down. The intersection there represents one of the most fascinating departures from the gridlock pattern of the city of Chicago's streets: It is a six-way thoroughfare with the Skyway hovering above. Seventy-Ninth Street runs east and west, Stony Island runs north and south, and S. Chicago Avenue runs on a diagonal, southeast and northwest.

Our office received a claim one day where the carrier who hired us had an insured that was in the concert promotional business. This theater I had loved so had become a Jehovah's Witness hall, and they apparently rented it out for concerts to augment their income. Our client, who was a promoter, had booked a rap group who had a reputation for having some unruly fans. The promoter had signed a contract guaranteeing that they would leave the premises in the same condition in which they had found it, but the band had literally incited their fans to riot with suggestive lyrics about disrespect for anyone in authority and property in general. The contract also called for the promoter to provide security. They provided two unarmed security guards. Fortunately, no one was killed or seriously hurt.

The first three rows, consisting of 75 seats, had been destroyed—they were the original seats installed when the theater was built, the same seats I had sat in so many times. We found a company in Michigan that restored or replicated theater seating, but the cost was outrageous at more than $600 a seat. I suggested that the carrier pay the loss, and then turn around and sue the band for its complicity in starting the riot. The promoter didn't like the idea too much, but suit was filed anyway. The band lost the suit, and ended up reimbursing the insurance carrier for 90 percent of the money paid out.

We were fortunate enough to find a couple of concert-goers who spoke to us in a forthright manner about the band egging the crowd on to destroy the place. Oddly enough, no one was ever arrested in the incident. According to the honest witnesses, the concert hadn't lasted the entire 90 minutes; it had been aborted at the halfway point, when the riot started.

Teenagers may look like adults, but under certain circumstances, particularly when in groups, they behave very badly. Statistics say it best: drunk driving, gun play, drug use, theft, property destruction, and even homicide are acts indulged in by teenagers every day. There's a reason auto insurance coverage is so high for young adults.

I never liked to sit in the first three rows when watching a movie anyway.

The Nanny

It is not unusual for an expectant mother to make arrangements to have an au pair, or a babysitter, come to the home to help care for a first newborn. When Jane Fleming, a new mother, hired a woman to care for her new daughter, she found her through an agency in the Yellow Pages. She queried several different agencies and checked references. The nanny who arrived appeared to be kind, nurturing, helpful and resourceful employee.

After having been home from the hospital for several days, Jane left the nanny alone with the most precious thing she had ever held dear. Less than two hours later, she arrived home and everything seemed to be fine. As the days passed, she began to trust the nanny and she felt comfortable leaving her baby with her. After a month or so, though, she found less need for the nanny's services. The baby was starting to sleep more regularly, and she now required only three days of service a week, then two, and then none at all. Nothing seemed out of the ordinary until a month passed and Jane found out that her credit card and license had been used to apply for credit at a very expensive stereo equipment store. She immediately suspected the nanny, but she was long gone by then. Jane wondered how she'd been able to get a hold of her Visa card and driver's license in the first place, and she began to feel ill at ease about having left her baby with this seemingly sweet individual. In fact, she became angst-ridden over the idea.

I entered the picture when a fidelity and surety claim was made by the store to get their money back from the insurance company for the value of the equipment, which had been purchased illegally. If I could, I wanted to identify the thief so that I could pursue reimbursement. When I found the nanny, I was surprised to meet a pretty, petite, blue-eyed blonde. She looked like a graduate from the Brady Bunch. Turns out she was also involved in a ring that was fencing stolen property. She had a drug habit to support
__________________ freebasing cocaine.

A police detective in Highland Park told me a good deal about the case. A male employee of the stereo store had become smitten with the phony nanny, though their contact was very brief. He had, himself, even delivered some hi-fi equipment that day to an apartment in Highland Park, though it was not the address on the application, which corresponded to the driver's license. In fact, Jane Fleming and the nanny did share a general resemblance, but there were obvious differences. This male employee, who had since quit his job, would not talk to us, and the police couldn't prove conclusively that he was in cahoots with the theft ring. It occurred to me that maybe he was just plain stupid. His manager surmised that the fellow's intention was an amorous relationship with the pretty young thief---she was obviously quite a flirt. A warrant was issued for her arrest in Colorado. They wanted her extradited for being involved in a similar scheme where several stores had been bilked out of merchandise to the tune of $175,000.

I met the phony nanny in Cook County Jail. She told me everything, including the fact that she had a 3-year-old daughter whom her mother was caring for. She also admitted that she had gone through severe withdrawals after being deprived of cocaine. She had, however, now found God, and she felt she was still young enough to reclaim her innate goodness.

Visiting Cook County Jail was an absolute delight. Because I wasn't the girl's attorney, I wasn't able to see her in a private room—I had to communicate with her by phone, with a glass partition separating us. Nearby, a very loud-mouthed guy talking to his brother was making quite a scene. Unable to mask his disbelief that his brother had been incarcerated for drug use, he excoriated his brother by calling him every derogatory name I have ever heard. He was so loud, I could hardly hear the sad story of the nanny who was trying to convince me that she was on the road to reclamation. Just before I left, the two brothers' mother entered and started in on her son as well in an equally boisterous and emotional manner.

When I left the jail, I actually used alcohol wipes to wash my hands and left ear where I'd made contact with the phone. I had a ringing headache, and I needed a good strong drink or instant amnesia to deal with what I'd just been through. The fun wasn't over yet, though. As I waited to retrieve my belongings from the jailers, I was propositioned by a Caucasian woman who was there to visit a prostitute who had been jailed for arson. She'd set fire to her pimp's apartment building. I must admit, this gal had a beautiful body, but her face had a major excess of mileage on it.

I'd been to the Criminal Courts Building at 26th and California on business quite a few times, but only to the Cook County jail three times. The first time had been on a field trip in high school. The second time had been to see the nanny, and the third was to visit a guy who was in jail for reckless homicide ___ he'd fled the scene of a fatal accident. The bail had been set very high and he couldn't raise the money to spring himself. My purpose there was to clear up a few salient points about whether he had had tacit permission to drive the car, which he had used to mow down a pedestrian. At the time, I was training a young woman to be an investigator, and we had traveled to the county jail as part of her indoctrination. Visiting hours were from 12:00 p.m. to 4:00 p.m. on Wednesday, for one hour only, because I was not an attorney. I was considered a regular Joe and I had to play by the public rules.

After arriving early, we had waited for 45 minutes before we were let into an area with several other visitors, Plexiglas bifurcating us, the innocent parties, from the hardened criminals. They had locked us in and, naturally, this rather sullen prisoner refused to talk. In fact, he told me to go "fuck myself" after I explained why I wanted to talk to him. I used the intercom to ask the guard to release us, but they would not respond. The air was stifling in there, and we felt very much like we were incarcerated ourselves for over an hour before we were let out. I was furious, but I had to forget about it. When you get poor service from a business, or a mistake in an order from a restaurant for carry out, that business sometimes gives out a gift certificate to create good will. With this in mind, I wrote to the warden hoping I'd get a special pass and parking privileges, which, of course, I never received. The only saving grace from that fiasco was that the insurance company paid me handsomely for my extra effort.

Back to the tale of the nanny, I learned she'd had two accomplices, and she gave me three or four aliases for one of them. The second fellow was her husband, who was on the lam with sever-al warrants out for his arrest. I never found the ringleader, how-ever, and the police didn't feel they had enough evidence to implicate him, even though he had been living in the apartment where the stereo equipment had been delivered by the infatuated but loose-tongued hi-fi salesman. Apparently, he'd moved from Highland Park to downtown Chicago and had melted into the masses. I was never able to talk to him.

The insurance company paid the store for the loss, and never got a penny back. The nanny ended up in a state prison in Colorado for six and a half years. The stereo equipment was never retrieved. Jane Fleming, the woman who had hired the nanny, filed suit against both the nanny service and concocted a theory of negligence against the stereo store, alleging that they hadn't scrutinized the driver's license closely enough. As regards the nanny service, Fleming complained that they hadn't made sufficient background checks before they'd hired and recommended a thief. Though there wasn't a pecuniary loss by Fleming, I believed she had a particularly good chance of nailing the nanny service for a gross breach of duty and trust, akin to negligent entrustment. As with many of my cases, when my own job was over, I was left out of the loop. I never did find out the outcome of the suits.

How can the need to carefully check and recheck credentials and backgrounds be illustrated more powerfully. This was a woman hired to care for a baby—the most precious thing imaginable. Had she infiltrated the family over a period of time, who knows what could have resulted? The child might well have been in imminent danger.

Never Out of Sight

I will never forget a unique case with hideous consequences on which I was forced to work with an attorney I knew for his questionable tactics. This time, he was representing a 10-year-old boy who had been a victim of sodomy, both orally and anally. The boy had been at a birthday party hosted by the parents of a school friend. He'd wandered away from the party, into an alley, and had been picked up by a deranged Hispanic man who took him to a forest preserve less than ten minutes away and raped him.

The party had begun in the afternoon, and there were four events involved: roller skating, pizza for dinner, "night cosmic" bowling, and finally, a sleepover. Eight boys were in attendance. The young victim had asked, between consuming pizza and bowling, if he could put on his roller blades and go out into the alley. The host lived close to a large city park, a block away or less, and he was at home supervising the boys. He told the boy to stay close. From his vantage point, the adult had a fairly clear view of the alley, which was in a middle-class neighborhood, with some nice properties, but not ostentatious. I would characterize it as a decent place to raise children. If I had been the parents, though, I never would have allowed a small child out of my sight in any neighborhood. Just two blocks to the west, there was a poorer neighborhood plagued by a high crime rate. While the boy's friend's mother was out buying breakfast food, the father lost sight of the victim when he was forced to referee a dispute between two other boys.

The victim wandered off down the alley, partially obscured from view because of the insured's garage, going eastbound (at least that is where we think he went), which was in the direction of the park. He was out of sight for perhaps five minutes. Almost immediately, the father realized he couldn't find the boy, and he enlisted the help of a few neighbors. They went all over the area without success. Frantic with worry, he did not call the boy's parents or the police right away. Later on, the boy showed up at his own house. He'd apparently walked home from wherever the rapist had dropped him off.

We later learned that the same rapist had tried to kidnap a woman a couple of hours earlier on the same day. The little boy had been taken in broad daylight, and returned to the same neighborhood at dusk. He had pleaded with the rapist not to kill him, and it may never be known what the rapist's ultimate intentions were. I was told that when the boy spoke to the police, he had explained that he'd talked about his love of Jesus and God, apparently making some impression on the rapist with his fervent and unshakable faith. It must have been by some quirk that the rapist dropped him off so close to his home.

The rapist was caught by the police that night. He had one item on his criminal record: a breaking and entering charge. He was 20 years old and out of work. The woman he had tried to attack had reported the incident to the police immediately, and they were actively looking for the rapist, not knowing that he had kidnapped a second victim. As it turns out, someone had witnessed the abduction and had called the police, but they hadn't taken her call seriously. They later alleged that they thought she was describing the first attempt the rapist had made a couple of hours earlier.

At 8:15 p.m., the police informed the party hosts that the boy was home. They had finally called the police themselves after searching for 20 minutes. The police arrived at their home to search it carefully, and then returned a half hour later to report that the boy was safe. The boy's parents were understandably upset, but it took a couple of days for their full fury to manifest itself. Within a month of the terrible event, my lawyer "friend" had started writing frightening letters to the party hosts, telling them that there was a possibility they could lose all their assets, including their home, because of their negligence. He wanted to know about their insurance coverage and what the liability limits were.

He asked all sorts of pointed questions: how much equity did they have in their home? Where did they work? How much money did they have in the bank? Had it been me, 1 would have responded by telling him where to get off. The two letters he sent were grandiose examples of why the public has such a sour and jaded opinion of attorneys in general. I think in his first life, this attorney was in charge of devising and expediting punitive measures and collecting reparations after World War I or maybe in another time and place he was one of the rapacious participants the macabre scene captured by the

Flemish painter Hieronymus Bosch in "Garden of Earthly Delights.

When I was asked to investigate, I called the parents who had hosted the party and I attempted to assuage their fears. They had not hired their own attorney, and they were planning to rely on their insurance company to fight their battles for them. What came out in the investigation was that the father had lost sight of the victim for a few minutes. The parents had been in charge of the children, and they were responsible for their safety and well-being. In fact, the mother worked in the law enforcement field, and she had a particularly acute under-standing of the repercussions of the case. Yet she wrote a letter to the editor of the local newspaper, bearing her soul about the incident. I remember thinking that she'd done so to partially mitigate her own guilt, and also to answer her critics in the neighborhood. What she wrote was pretty damning, though, and impossible to overcome from a liability standpoint. She'd admitted everything, including the fact that her husband had lost sight of the victim, and that neither the police nor the boy's parents had been called right away. Notwithstanding the feelings or emotional fallout of the victim and his parents, the parents that held the party were absolutely devastated.

I know exactly why the attorney wrote the letters as he did—it was to elicit an immediate response from the insurance carrier. The letters had their desired effect. The attorney wanted to try and settle, short of filing suit, if he could. The policy limit was $300,000. The attorney asked for the limit, and after a minor degree of red tape, he got it.

The little boy will be in counseling for a very long time. Perhaps he'll find out one day that he was never at fault, and perhaps he can learn to live a productive life without all of the baggage that occurs as a result of a tragic happenstance such as this.

CHAPTER 5: BEHIND THE WHEEL

Car accidents are all too common, and the results can change, or end, lives. In my line of work, I've been involved in the investigation of multiple collisions, fender-benders, catapulted bodies, pedestrian pitfalls, and some very horrific injuries. While it's possible to become jaded after years in the business, there are some cases that will never leave my memory bank.

LSD

I've never run across Lake Shore Drive (LSD) that I can remember. I have never been silly stupid drunk when attempting to dodge speeding projectiles. I have run across lanes of an inter-state after taking photos while doing an investigation on an auto case, though. When a truck is coming at you at 60 miles an hour, most people have a compelling reason to get out of the way. Over the past 27 years, I have had two cases involving people being hit on Lake Shore Drive; both were on the north side.

Before I recount the sordid details of these two cases, allow me to extol the virtues of the city of Chicago and its Lake Front and skyline. Lake Shore Drive runs south of the downtown area, and north of the downtown area. It provides a gorgeous view of Chicago, all the way from the Museum of Science and Industry on the south end to Hollywood Boulevard on the north end. The views of the skyline and Lake Michigan are spectacular. A ride down Lake Shore Drive on a clear day, especially when the sun is rising, can lift almost anyone's spirits. There are several beaches and parks east of the drive, and on nice summer days, particularly on weekends, people congregate in groups all over. Huge amounts of alcohol, and other things, are consumed on a regular basis.

For those who have not been to Chicago, Lake Michigan is 120 miles wide, and you cannot see across it unless you have wings. The city's museums are all unique structures that rival any in the world. Most are on the lakefront, except for the Art Institute, which is not run by the city of Chicago. The Aquarium and Oceanarium are sandwiched between Monroe Harbor and

Burnham Harbor. The Planetarium is a little bit farther south and east of the Aquarium. Well south is the Museum of Science and Industry at 57th Street, and we must not forget the Field Museum, which is just north of Soldier Field.

For those who do not stray off the beaten track, and stay close to the downtown area and Lake Shore Drive, Chicago is a very beautiful and exquisitely laid-out city. The neighborhoods, in general, are uncluttered and clean, at least in recent years. Mayor Daley has done a yeoman's job of enhancing the neighborhoods. I find that Chicago has every advantage of a large diverse urban area, without the arrogance and chill that characterizes a city like New York. Sure, New York is a bit more electric than Chicago, and it's a town that never sleeps, but I'll take Chicago any time. Our Midwestern charm is contagious.

The first case involving the hazards of LSD concerned a Honduran man, around 19 years of age, who did not speak English. He was running across Lake Shore Drive near Lawrence Avenue because some girl's jealous boyfriend was going to puncture his aorta with a large carving knife. He was running from the park just south of the viaduct (there is a walkway underneath the drive), and he made it across the northbound lanes okay, but he was hit by a car in the southbound lanes. He suffered a fractured femur and right clavicle. I took a Spanish-speaking court reporter with me to Louis Weiss Hospital to interview him. He told us the whole story.

The man had only been in town for a few weeks. I later heard through the grapevine that he was going to be deported. In other words, he had crossed through our border from Mexico illegally. The hospital couldn't wait to jettison him, because they were never going to see a dime. I contacted the Chicago police officer who had investigated the accident, and inquired about the man's status as a U.S. resident. He was found to have no legal status. The police officer actually referred to him as a "border jumper."

I left the hospital as surreptitiously as possible. I didn't want them to get any ideas about the driver's insurance carrier paying any of the illegal alien's bills. If they had asked, I would have denied their lien outright. This fellow was clearly a pretty enterprising individual to make it all the way to Chicago from Honduras. Under different circumstances, I would like to have quizzed him about his experiences on such a long and undoubtedly perilous journey. I even considered submitting a magazine article about him that would have made for some interesting reading. Regrettably, his story did not have a happy ending.

An establishment serving liquor in a bar or restaurant is required by law to have liquor liability coverage called dram shop coverage. Prior to 1986, one could secure a contribution from a dram shop carrier if they were faced with a third-party claim from an innocent party struck by an insured who had been over-served alcohol. Lake Shore Drive is a focal point here because one particular over- served patron, who was down near Rush Street at a famous place in the nightclub district just north of downtown Chicago, somehow staggered to his automobile and made it several blocks over to North Avenue without nailing any pedestrians or other cars. At the North Avenue exit for south-bound traffic, this guy tried to get onto Lake Shore Drive going northbound—only he was using the southbound exit ramp. He hit someone, but not quite head-on, because the driver getting off Lake Shore Drive steered to her right, even though she was blinded by the fellow's headlights.

The attorney for the injured woman let me take her statement. Her injuries were not of a permanent nature, so eventually the case was settled for $14,000. Incredibly, the drunk driver who hit her got out of the car after the crash and walked over to her before she could move, casually asking if there was any way they could handle the situation without calling the police. Both cars were destroyed and the woman's car had jumped the curb to her right and ended up on the grass.

The intoxicated driver was charged with DUI. As his carrier's representative, I contacted the dram shop carriers for the two bars where he had been for the majority of the evening and into the wee hours of the morning. I was able to get them to pay $6,000 of the $14,000 settlement.

In 1986, the Dram Shop Act was altered to prohibit such contributions. The third party, however, could go after the dram shop carrier unilaterally, in addition to any third party claim they had against the drunk driver. The liquor liability laws are written to protect an innocent party from the actions of an over-served individual, and it is incumbent on the bar owner to be careful about anyone who has had one too many. Of course, when a bar is crowded, particularly on a Friday or Saturday night, the bartender is like a whirling dervish, serving drinks and hearing the sweet music of the cash register ringing. Picking out that over-served person is not always the first priority.

Another incident of note involving Lake Shore Drive (LSD) revolved around a young couple running across LSD in broad daylight. Again, the impact occurred in the southbound lanes. They were both underage and had been drinking near Diversey Harbor. It was a beautiful day to be on the lakefront.

There is a jogging path just east of the northbound lanes. Multiple signs posted warn pedestrians that crossing Lake Shore Drive is strictly verboten. This couple had to climb over a three and a half foot retaining wall. If they made it safely to the middle of the roadway, an island with a terrace of flowers and shrubbery had to be traversed before they could then try to make it across the southbound lanes. Ironically, not far from where they attempted to cross, there was a pedestrian tunnel going under the drive, which would have kept them from harm. The fact that they went the long and dangerous route makes one wonder if they were some kind of thrill seekers. They both had high levels of alcohol in their bloodstreams—the man had a reading of .27, and the woman had a reading of .24. They were both killed when they ran in front of a car going 45 to 50 miles per hour in a 45- mile an hour speed zone.

The driver of the car had no chance to avoid the tragedy, as the couple had darted out, going east to west from the island in the middle of the roadway, when the automobile was less than two car lengths away. Witnesses said that the driver was not speeding. They also agreed that he had no chance, even though he had applied his brakes before impact. The front end of the car caught both of them flush. The girl flew off the car sideways; it was miraculous that she wasn't hit by yet another car. The boy went up over the hood and roof and was struck by another vehicle that was attempting to stop. Both were transported to a nearby hospital and were pronounced dead upon arrival. Observers said that there was no sign of life for either party at the scene of the accident.

Both families hired attorneys. I told both attorneys that we were taking a very dim view of the case. If the cases were to be tried, I was sure the driver would be declared not guilty. Funeral costs being expensive, the carrier agreed to make an offer to each attorney to resolve the matter without having to incur legal costs. I settled each case for $10,000-this represented more than a nuisance value settlement, and it provided a solution for all involved, except the dead. The solution precluded ending up with a legal bill of $30,000, and vitiated any chance of a jury in Cook County running amok and awarding some unreasonable figure.

Tragedy on the North Side

It was 10 below zero in early February. The wind chill was 30 below. Traffic was light, and a hardworking woman at a well-known hospital on the north side of Chicago was crossing a normally busy street at 9 p.m. to catch a CTA bus to go home. She weighed no more than 145 pounds, lived with her son, and rode 30 minutes to get home, changing buses once to get closer to her apartment. She was wearing dark clothing and had a bag with her. She tried to cross going from south to north, east of the traffic light, and not in the crosswalk. In fact, she was at least 10 or 15 feet east of the crosswalk.

To enter the street, she had to step down from a curb and slip between two parked cars. Why she didn't cross at the intersection is unknown, and why she didn't see the eastbound car coming is a mystery as well. Maybe she did see the car coming and did something rash, but I don't think so. It appeared as if she walked right in front of the car, which was going 30 miles per hour. The front of the car caught her flush, flipping her up into the air. She landed on the pavement, in the westbound lane, several feet east of where she had been trying to cross.

The fellow who hit her, a quiet and unassuming type, was new to the Chicago area. He related to me in our interview that he was having a hard time sleeping—he was devastated by the tragedy. I reassured him that there was nothing he could have done to avoid it; his headlights were both working and he hadn't seen her, though he'd felt the impact, which he described as being like hitting a deer.

The woman had been taken to a local hospital where they'd tried desperately to save her life over a period of 18 hours. She died at the hospital the next day. The report showed that they had injected her with experimental drugs, and that at death, she had weighed more than 240 pounds. At first I wondered if they were even referring to the same woman. The bill was $59,000.

I never got a satisfactory explanation as to why she had spontaneously gained so much weight. Maybe it was a typographical error, but I doubt it. The insurance coverage was only $100,000, and liability was highly questionable. She had stepped in front of a vehicle going 30 miles per hour in an area which was not well lit, but she was nowhere near a crosswalk, and had crossed against the light.

Infarction on the Road

No insurance carrier will pay a claim for property damage or bodily injury when it is due to an auto accident caused by a medical emergency such as a stroke, a heart attack, or a seizure, if it can be proven that the emergency could not be reasonably expected. I once had a case where a diabetic doctor had caused a terrible accident because he hadn't eaten properly, nor had he taken his insulin. He admitted himself that he had been in classic, old-fashioned diabetic shock. We could not depend on, or use, the sudden emergency defense, because in the course of two years, this same doctor had caused four such accidents while operating a motor vehicle in an insulin-deprived stupor. This doctor had continually passed out at the wheel, causing hair-raising accidents. There is no defense for a repeat of such incidents.

Case Law in Illinois relies on the premise that a sudden medical emergency is not an event to be expected. It is an act of God. This is perfectly illustrated in a case concerning a 27-year-old salesman, George Sanders, who was making $35,000 a year back in 1977, a great salary for anyone at that time, especially for a fellow of his age. As George was on his way in the car from one sales call to another, he inexplicably had a heart attack, rendering him incapable of controlling the vehicle. Subsequently, he crashed into two cars, smashed through the bushes of someone's front yard, and ended up with his front bumper in their living room.

Sanders had been through a physical ordered by his new employer six months before the accident, and had been declared to be in excellent health. He didn't smoke and, by all accounts, he drank sparingly. His co-workers reported that he loved his job and was genuinely enthusiastic about his future. Clearly, he was not a candidate for stress-related health problems. There was no history of heart disease in his family, and he took no medication for any condition. But George Sanders died in the process of the heart attack and ensuing car crash.

The coroner performed an autopsy. The cause of death was listed as a heart attack; the automobile accident was listed as secondary. The question remained, however: this fellow _______ an otherwise healthy, happy and athletic individual ______ was the last person this sort of tragedy should have befallen. All factors pointed toward his living a long life. In any case where it could be shown that there were factors to support that an event was unexpected, the carrier would not be obliged to pay the claims. The claims emanating from the accident were denied, supported by the sudden medical emergency defense. It was important that a very thorough investigation be done. Unless the carrier could show unequivocally that it had been a true emergency, they had to show good faith and pay the claims.

During a different case, I dealt with an attorney who simply refused to understand my argument regarding this doctrine. I sent him the appropriate case law regarding the issue, which was laid out in a chronological order, citing older cases right on through present ones. All of these cases were consistent on the matter; they indicated that a true sudden medical emergency merited a declination of the claim. The attorney had a client who was a longstanding friend of the driver and had been a passenger on the day of the accident. I had taken this woman's statement before she had hired the attorney, and she told me that her friend had been healthy, he hadn't been taking any medication, and he hadn't seen a doctor recently. He'd had a heart attack at the wheel and had lost control of the vehicle, which flipped over several times. Quite horrific __ for the man had been decapitated as he'd been ejected from the car.

When an autopsy was performed, it was clear that the man had suffered from a heart attack, or "cardiac arrest," as the record stated. The woman had answered my questions honestly and without knowledge of the issues at hand. The claim was quickly denied based on a sudden medical emergency doctrine and subsequent defense. The attorney tried to make an uninsured motorist's case with her carrier, which was also denied.

Educating the lower echelon attorney is always satisfying. Personal injury attorneys are the scourge of the legal profession, though there are a few good ones out there. 1 made it abundantly clear that this attorney simply did not know the law or the issues of the case. He was clearly a rank amateur when it came to this type of law. I believe his main practice involved handling real estate closings. He was out of his league.

He Felt Just Fine

Within this same realm of scenarios, there is another case worth mentioning. Three to four months before he died of a heart attack behind the wheel, a man in his late 50s visited his doctor complaining of shortness of breath and general fatigue. The doctor wanted to order various tests, but our victim never returned to have them done. According to his wife, who gave us a consent form to view his medical records, he really didn't want to know what was wrong with him. He didn't smoke, he only occasionally consumed alcoholic beverages, and he was, by all accounts, a healthy specimen. By the time he made that first visit to the doctor, he had been suffering from flu-like symptoms and a cold for four months.

The gentleman's employer would not let me interview his co-workers, and his supervisor cut me off short after answering very few questions. While I was in his office, however, the supervisor received a call from one of his bosses in regard to being pursued by the man's widow. The deceased had helped run a warehouse operation and in the months before his death, he had been through an especially stressful period. After a particularly difficult day, he lost control of his car after having a heart attack and hit two parked cars, one of which was occupied. Then, he'd gone over the center divider and hit a third car head-on, causing severe injuries to the lone driver, who survived after being on life support for a period of weeks, racking up tremendous medical bills.

I would have liked to have been able to see the records from the physical the deceased man's employer made mandatory on a yearly basis, but the employer refused to release them. Perhaps it had been a cursory exam without much to go on, but I would never know. The carrier, my principal, had a very hard decision to make. Would they deny or address the third-party claims?

When I had asked the man's wife to sign the medical authorization form, I had quizzed her about his health. She answered that she knew nothing, or that she had been advised to say nothing. I surmised that someone had counseled her to say she didn't know. She claimed that she'd been under the impression that he was healthy before he died—he'd never complained about anything being wrong. She knew he had been to the doctor, and that he'd been treated for his flu and cold symptoms, and that was that. He had apparently never mentioned any shortness of breath to her, and she was unaware of any undue duress he was experiencing at work. Either she was lying, or he'd given her the silent treatment.

The stakes were high in this case. The fellow had a $500,000 liability limit on his policy, but the investigation was inconclusive. The employer would not release the health records, even with the authorization. "You will only get these by subpoena," they'd said.

In general, the employer had taken a very hard stance on the case because of potential workers' compensation exposure. A smart attorney might have been able to prove the heart attack had been induced by stress created on the job, and they weren't taking any chances. In order to prove a heart attack is subject to compensation, it must be proven that working conditions are so stressful that a heart attack might likely result. The fact that people in their 40s or 50s often have heart attacks, for a variety of reasons, cannot be used as an excuse that none of these claims are compensable. Poor eating habits, lack of exercise, bad genes, a predisposition to heart problems, and stress all contribute to this end result.

One factor that can be linked to the possibility that a heart attack is job-related is stress, which can result from working too much, for too many hours, at too frenetic a pace, with endless deadlines, or dealing with people who make your blood boil. Sometimes not getting along with superiors can lead to situations resulting in undeniable stress. Co-workers can contribute to stress when there are major personality conflicts. Lastly, constant and unpredictable change in the work environment can lead to emotional problems contributing to stress.

From a worker's compensation standpoint, one must be very circumspect in his/her approach on these cases; external factors may significantly outweigh on-the-job considerations. Typically, a heart attack allegedly caused by stress is more likely to be a result of factors that are not job-related, including diet, exercise, sleep habits, marital difficulties, financial problems and overbearing children. These are all bona fide, salient reasons why people have heart attacks, and none of them have anything to do with one's career. Proving a compensable claim as a result of heart attack is a great hurdle to leap, and an attorney taking on such a case will have an especially hard time if the victim has not been exposed to a high-octane, stress-filled occupation.

Health records are crucially important sources of information, particularly because many claimants have selective memories when it comes to past medical histories. In other words, many people lie about their past heart problems. Many heart attack victims don't die, and are able to make full, or at least partial, recoveries. Beware of the heart attack victim who claims to have been in perfect health with no symptoms. Nine times out of ten, the investigation will reveal the truth.

The fellow with the huge amount of medical bills ended up with his claim being denied based on the sudden emergency doctrine defense. His family secured the services of an attorney. Suit was filed and the case is still pending.

Bliss of Matrimony

I don't know if this qualifies as a sudden medical emergency __ it certainly wasn't perceived as such when it happened in the 1970s ____ but a very nice man, Joseph Santini, was in a very bad automobile accident after he blacked out at the wheel. On the night of the accident, Mr. Santini had been coming home from his nephew's birthday party. He had had a couple of drinks, but he was not legally intoxicated. Nevertheless, he blacked out. When questioned later, he hadn't an inkling of what had occurred. Witnesses, though, had seen him go over the center dividing line, and he had hit someone head-on at 45 miles per hour. The result was a fractured right femur, several broken ribs and a collapsed lung. Luckily, he recovered nicely. The lady he hit never recovered. She was put on life support and died within five weeks.

Santini related his sad story to me one evening in 1977. Two months before the accident, he had found his best friend with his wife of 35 years in his own bedroom. Santini was a butcher by trade and appeared to be a strait-laced, hardworking Christian man. He gave the appearance of goodness and simplicity ____ the antithesis of flamboyance. Maybe his wife had become bored with him. Immediately after his "discovery," his wife moved out with his best friend, leaving her husband emotionally bereft. He became despondent. Of course, the accident only made matters worse for him. In the course of my work, I have never had such a strong desire to just reach out and hug someone, and I remembered to include him in a prayer, which is something I seldom do.

Lost Commission

A famous sports agent I worked with had no scruples. His attitude was: if you could take advantage of a situation, you were an idiot not to avail yourself of the opportunity, regardless of morals. His theory was, "My mama didn't raise me to be a chump." I know that in public, he wouldn't have put it exactly in those terms, but that was about the size of it. In my line of work, I've found that some people look at every transaction in life as a contest, and it is imperative that they win.

The agent's car, a Mercedes 600, had been tapped from behind, and a front license plate holder had scratched his rear bumper. The repair cost $2,500, which the carrier paid. That should have been the end of it, but the agent claimed that he and his wife had both been hurt. She had never gone to see a doctor, but her husband alleged that she had lost income. Unfortunately, he paid her cash to help him in his business, and he had no records to substantiate her loss.

When I met him at his two-million dollar home on the North Shore, he told me he'd seen three different doctors, one of whom treated injured football players. He alleged that he had a bulging disk in the lumbar spine as a result of the impact of the fender-scratcher. The accident had happened at the end of July, and he claimed to have been disabled for a week after. During this time, he claimed he'd lost out on signing football players to handle their contract negotiations because he was unable to travel from team to team at their training facilities and meet with players. He said he'd lost over $50,000 in potential income as a result. He also said he had about $1,500 in medical bills, but one of the doctors who treated him had not actually charged him.

My principal, an insurance carrier, was liquidating their business, and they simply wanted his case settled. They had stopped writing new policies in Illinois and Wisconsin, and they weren't terribly concerned about how much money it would cost. I was handling the entire run off claims, which are policies already on the books when they decided to shut down, for them, and they were actually overpaying claims routinely just to get the business off the books. Someone at the insurance company had made this fellow an $18,000 offer—which was rejected—and I had to do my best to settle the case for $22,000, in reference to his injury. They wanted his wife's case settled for $500.

Well, this guy must have thought we were a bunch of idiots, and he treated me as if I was one of the hired hands in his house.

While I was there, I sat around for a while as he answered telephone calls. It reminded me of the old television ads where a guy picked up the phone line, ordering, "Chicago, sell! New York, sell! San Francisco, sell!" I wasn't feeling traumatized when I left, but paying out what he received certainly wasn't my idea. The way he treated me, and the way the carrier treated him, ran completely against my professional claim-handling instincts. I didn't like it one bit. If it were up to me, I would have told him from the outset that we would fix his car and give him $500 to walk, or he could go ahead and file suit and see what a jury would have to say. Like most agents, this fellow was a real smooth talker, but I was confident that some people, at least, could see through his veneer. His arrogance was atrocious and reprehensible, and the carrier should have made him work a hell of a lot harder for the money he got.

When an offer is made on a claim, even if it is rejected, the carrier is hard pressed to backtrack on that offer at a later date, no matter how much they might protest. The offer is withdrawn if rejected, and everyone goes back to square one, meaning zero, in theory that is. Short of sending a case to a jury, the other side will harp on that one time offer forever. If a jury awards an amount lower than a previous offer submitted in the course of a negotiation, that is about the only way to renege on that offer. Insurance companies don't want to be embroiled in bad faith actions, because there is a distinct and strong possibility that they might end up paying out more than the liability limit, which is the worst thing that can happen to an insurance carrier. Blood and bile boil when that happens.

Dead Men Don't Talk

A fellow driving a delivery truck down Racine Avenue claimed that he had a green light at Taylor Street. He was going southbound, which was his line of travel. Another fellow in an older BMW, with no collision coverage on his car, claimed that he had the green light, going east on Taylor Street. He had hit the passenger side of the truck, whose cab and cargo areas were one unit —a straight job truck—pretty hard, because the truck flipped over on the driver's side. Both parties were injured, but not seriously.

The insured driver gave a decent statement, sticking to his story about having the green light. It was plausible enough, especially after he mentioned a witness, a lady friend of his who happened to be standing on the corner. I didn't get a lot of detail from her, though—she related the same basic account as our driver did. But there was another witness who lived in a high-rise public housing building just south of St. Ignatius. The problem was, he wouldn't talk to us. When I tried to meet with him, he didn't show up. I called him over a period of six months, but he never responded.

At first, the claimant was not represented, but when we refused to pay for the damage to his car, he became impatient and hired a middle-of-the-road law firm. The attorney who handled the case for him was the non-communicative type. I called him more than 30 times and wrote several times, but I received no feedback whatsoever. I threatened to close our file, but before I did, I warned that I would contact his client to make sure his wishes were being fulfilled. This ploy elicited a verbal outpouring of such monumental proportions, I realized that I could no longer deem him the silent type. It really didn't change anything, and it occurred to me that this attorney had no game plan on the case to begin with. Actually, I was hoping that they would file suit so that we could at least move forward. He would not send my office any bills or records, and he would not furnish me with a medical authorization form.

A couple of months before the bodily injury statute was about to expire, I contacted the insured, a delivery service. The principal told me something that startled me: our driver, who wasn't exactly an old man, had apparently passed away. Immediately, I reassessed the situation, realizing that without witnesses, the plaintiff would never be able to prove his case. Still, I called the attorney, only to find out that there had been another startling development. The attorney who had taken such exception to my amateur ploy to shake him into some type of action had left the firm. Now I could make some headway. I talked to one of the firm partners and told him I would like to see the medical bills, medical records, and the lost wages records. He sent them three weeks before the statute ran out, and I perused them and sent them on to the insurance company. They gave me $5,000 in authority to settle, which was summarily rejected. Prior to that I asked a couple of times if the law firm had ever contacted the witness listed on the police report. They had been unable to roust him.

Soon, they filed suit, and I received an angry call from the plaintiff's attorney asking me where they could find the driver of our truck. I reminded him that it was not our duty or responsibility to help him prove his case. Then I dropped a bomb shell: I told him our driver was dead, and he could secure a death certificate at Vital Records. The silence on the other end of the phone seemed endless. He obviously understood the implications, although I would have gleefully explained them.

Our lady on the corner, the one who claimed to be a witness, was now nowhere to be found. When I'd met with her previously, she wouldn't give me a social security number or her driver's license number, so I knew it was unlikely that she'd really seen anything. I'd had my doubts about her from the beginning, and I wasn't surprised by her disappearance. Furthermore, our driver wasn't around anymore to tell me where he'd found her in the first place. So, we had no witnesses, and the dead man's statute states clearly and concisely that neither combatant in litigation can testify against the other if one of the parties is no longer on the earth to provide a rebuttal. That, of course, would create an unfair advantage. If there is a preponderance of evidence, physical or otherwise, that might shed light on the matter contested, then it is allowed, of course.

The plaintiff had a pile of rubble and they knew it. They reluctantly accepted the $5,000 because they had no choice. I'm sure that it occurred to them that, as a firm, they were at risk in terms of their professional liability exposure because they had mismanaged the case. In my mind, they were, in some respects, unlucky. The original attorney handling the case, by lack of action, had set the tone for a losing proposition. It must have been a blow to be forced to accept just $5,000.

A Deer in the Headlight

When it comes to road accidents, one of the most unusual circumstances I ever encountered was when a mentally retarded woman rode down Ridge Road in Chicago on a bicycle with four large plastic bags of aluminum cans she had picked up at the lakefront parks on the north side. She was on a monumental scavenger hunt, apparently. It was a dark Sunday night, around 11:00 p.m., the temperature was in the low 50s, and there was a driving rainstorm. The woman was riding the wrong way on Ridge Road, going northbound in the southbound lane.

The driver who hit her was a fairly prominent attorney who was returning home from dropping off his mother, whom he'd had to his home for dinner. He'd had a couple of drinks earlier in the evening, but he was not intoxicated. He never saw her. The plastic bags were dark, as was her clothing, and she had no head-light. She had one reflector on the back end of the bike, but he had nailed her in the front. She suffered a fractured shoulder and humerus, a ruptured spleen, and torn cartilage in her knee as a result of the impact.

I went to see her at the hospital. I tried to interview her, but it was obvious that she was unable to communicate as a result of her mental illness. I got whatever information I could, and I left my business card. Two days later an attorney, whom I knew quite well, called. I took a written statement from the insured driver and sent it to the insurance company with my report. The woman was in the hospital for more than three weeks after surgery on her shoulder, knee and the removal of her spleen. (Without a spleen, a person is much less resistant to infection.) Her bills were more than $30,000, she really didn't have any income to speak of, and she had never filed a tax return at any point in her life.

Then, the attorney pulled a fast one on the carrier. He called the carrier during the lunch hour and asked the claims support girl, who isn't really a secretary, to send him a copy of the insured's statement, which was covered under a cloak of protection, or "privilege." The attorney for the injured woman couldn't have gotten that statement even if the Supreme Court had ordered it! But the claims support employee forwarded the statement unknowingly and ignorantly, and sent it to the attorney without even asking him who he represented. Maybe she thought that he was defense counsel, but she certainly should have asked her superior before doing so. Without the statement, the attorney would never have known that the insured had enjoyed a couple of drinks before the accident, even though his last drink had been at least two and a half hours before the accident. This was damaging, but I didn't believe it couldn't be overcome in the final analysis. The police report made no mention of our driver being impaired.

The problem was, we could win the battle and still lose the war. If the case had ever gone to trial, the attorney for the plain-tiff could not have used the information sent by the claims gal. The jury would never have heard about alcohol consumption on the part of the insured. The truth was, the attorney had stolen the information. If I had been the claims manager, or the director or vice president of claims, I would have fired that employee immediately, and I would have written a letter to the Attorney Registration and Disciplinary Commission (ARDC) complaining of fraud and deceit on the part of the attorney. My third move would have been to issue a directive never to settle a case with that attorney again, forcing him to file suit on any future case he might have with that particular insurance company. Maybe they knew something I didn't and weren't inclined to follow my suggestions.

The carrier settled the case for $140,000 within a week of the attorney receiving the damaging and illegally purloined statement. The medical records were not complete, but they decided to simply put the fire out. Was their driver really negligent? I think not. But they just couldn't take a chance with a jury. The policy limits were much higher than the payout that was made, and the perspective of a jury would most likely have been that the defendant had hit her head-on. Taking into consideration the fact that she was retarded, practically homeless and virtually helpless, the jury would no doubt have awarded her some serious cash. Incidentally the attorney, who engineered the settlement on behalf of his client, was disbarred about a year and a half later for improper solicitation of cases.

Cop Car

On New Year's Eve day in 1982, I arranged for a court reporter. At 8 a.m., we showed up at Cabrini Green to interview a young man, Tyrone Gunn, who was a key witness in a case I was investigating. He had been involved in an accident on Halsted, near Greek Town. The police had shown up and had issued him a tick-et. While they were there, their squad car had been pulverized on the back end by a motorist who drove as if he'd been semi-comatose. It happened in broad daylight.

The police claimed that they had been in the squad car at the time of impact, but the fellow they pulled over, who had been involved in another accident farther up the street, disputed that. He insisted that the police had been outside the squad car and out of harm's way. The driver of the vehicle that hit the police car wasn't any help—he was intoxicated and could not remember anything. He registered a .31 alcohol level in his bloodstream; it's no wonder he was hazy on the details. The accident had happened at 9:40 a.m. I took a statement from him and I was unable to garner any useful information about whether or not the officers had been in the squad car. All he wanted was to talk about his own injuries—he had been hospitalized for three weeks after demolishing the squad car.

The weather wasn't inclement on the last day of the year when we arrived at Cabrini Green, probably the most infamous housing project ever constructed. As a publicity stunt, the Mayor of Chicago, Jane Byrne, a white female, had lived there for a week in the early 1980s. On that day, it was 27 degrees, so no one was milling around. I was counting on that or I wouldn't have gone. We had to take a rickety slow, extremely noisy elevator up to the fifth floor. It seemed as if we'd never make it to our destination, and I was fearful that we might get stuck. When we finally made it to the fifth floor landing, the next trick was to find the correct apartment _______ over half the doors had no identifying letters or numbers. I knocked on three doors before we found the right one. Our star witness, though, wasn't up yet. His mama brought him to life with a severe verbal bar-rage and he came out of the back bedroom, dragging his rear end with a rather sheepish look on his face. It was clear from the get-go that neither Mama nor son had much regard for Chicago's finest. **In** spite of that, I was soon convinced that the witness was telling the truth about the gendarmes pending "vacancy" dilemma.

We sat on an old, beat-up, smelly sofa with diffuse light coming sparingly through the small holes in the threadbare blanket covering the main window. It appeared there was a 15-watt bulb in the ceiling socket, which provided the only artificial light in the entire apartment. My immediate inclination was to ask Mama to turn on a light in the living room area, which was located off the kitchen, but I saw a couple of roaches on the kitchen wall and thought better. I just wanted to get the hell out of there, and quick. Actually, I wanted to find a sanitization chamber.

The overgrown boy told us what we'd come to find out, and the plausibility of his account was enhanced when he told us that the cops had told him to wait by his car. It was as they were walking back to the squad car that the accident had happened.

The witness said they were walking in unison, 50 feet away from the squad car when it was smashed. The squad car had been in the middle of the southbound lane with the lights on, but with no siren.

Armed with this information, I threatened to go the office of professional standards if the attorney for the two cops would not cease and desist. He did, and we never paid a dime. When I got home later that day, I cleaned out my briefcase, pulled the pockets out of my pants and jacket to make sure that I hadn't imported any unwanted insects.

Calculating Costs

I met an attorney for the first time at the DuPage County Courthouse in January of 2000. I was there was to take a statement from a driver my carrier insured. It seemed to be a logical place to meet, because the driver was there to respond to a ticket he had received due to a bad accident. The passenger in the other car, a 60-year-old woman, suffered a fractured hip, which would eventually require a hip replacement. The attorney was trying to persuade our defendant, the insured driver, to enter a plea of guilty regarding the improper left-turn charge. Since the case had serious repercussions, the carrier sent counsel to represent the driver. It was a rather bold move for the attorney of the injured party to interfere with the driver of our car. This is a breach of etiquette, and was considered unethical behavior. He tried to steamroll the defense attorney, but was unsuccessful.

Our driver was from Taiwan, and seemed likely to be persuaded to do almost anything. I knew I was in for some serious negotiations with this attorney if, in fact, we could ever settle the case. He immediately wanted to know what the policy limits were, which I gave to him without making him adhere to the dictates of the Illinois statute regarding that issue. I made it plain that by divulging that information, I was in no way even hinting that we felt that this was a policy limits case. He provided copious medical records and reports--the major issue was how many hip replacements surgeries the injured woman would have to endure.

The attorney maintained that she would need to have at least two operations, because at 60, she would live to be at least 78. We found out that she was diabetic and insulin dependent, and I argued that her life expectancy did not compute to age 78. We had several discussions regarding the issue, and then I found some information in my Merck Manual, and by searching the Internet, which gave me a powerful rebuttal to his contentions. He made it plain: he wanted to settle the case. But he filed suit anyway, and I arranged for a 90-day extension. I negotiated with him, never having authority beyond $150,000, though his initial demand was $600,000. He eventually came down to $450,000, and then to $400,000. I came up from $75,000 to $135,000.

In the meantime, I had the woman's x-rays examined by a very well-respected orthopedic doctor in the west suburbs. According to him, she did, in fact, have a legitimate hip fracture. The story was that she hadn't had the surgical intervention immediately because she was from the West Coast. She had stayed in the hospital for two weeks, and then she'd gone home. She simply did not want to have major medical treatment in the Chicago area. Our doctor affirmed that she was a candidate for hip replacement surgery. With a relatively sedentary lifestyle, the hip replacement would last a long time, maybe even 20 years. Her own doctor's notes suggested that she was having a hell of a time adjusting to her lack of mobility. Her husband was forced to become her constant caretaker, requiring physical strength to help her move around. It required both time and patience.

We negotiated as this information about her condition was coming to us in bits and pieces. The attorney seemed to be stuck on settling the case for $310,000 to $325,000. When he realized that we were not going to bite, he did not become exasperated and pull the plug, however. I felt all along that the case had a value of $225,000, maybe a little more, maybe a little less. We were getting pretty close to the expiration of the extension of time to answer the lawsuit, but the attorney had not threatened to end negotiations. I realized at that point that $225,000 would be the number. We continued negotiations until I finally told the attorney that $250,000 would not be forthcoming--I had told the carrier that $225,000 was it. Finally, reality and judgment meshed and the case was settled for $225,000-a far distance from $600,000!

Illegal and Insane

Back in the late 1980s, there was a big push by the IRS to crack down on corporations or companies that utilized independent contractors as the core of their workforce. I specifically remember a catering business that treated drivers as independent contractors. In fact, the drivers were really salesmen, and they earned a percentage of what they sold. Often, they could be found parked outside a factory or construction site, where they would dispense sandwiches, doughnuts, coffee and soft drinks. Vendors at ballparks are also treated this way: they buy the merchandise they hawk and keep the profits. Independent contractors are responsible for paying their own taxes, and very often such taxes go unpaid, which is why the IRS was making a major effort to plug the hole.

In the Chicago area, the catering business is made up largely of Hispanic drivers. I've dealt with two major catering companies, and 99 percent of their workforce is Hispanic. Many of these individuals are here illegally, and incredibly enough, some of the workers have driver's licenses obtained through the black market. Some don't have licenses at all!

Catering truck driver Jaime Lopez had a legitimate license at one time, but it had been suspended, and his supervisor had never implemented the regular six-month check to be sure that all licenses were current. When an independent contractor uses a truck provided by the owner of a business profiting from the independent contractor's activity, there is an agency relationship in force. The independent contractor is an agent of the business.

Mr. Lopez was driving a catering truck on the north side of Chicago. He may or may not have run into a deranged Iranian fellow riding a bicycle. Allegedly, there were two witnesses, according to the police report, but neither one had seen the impact. Lopez said he was stopped, and the bicycle rider had run into the back of the truck, illegally parked in a bus stop zone. The bicycle rider was incoherent after the accident and he never offered or rendered a cogent account as to what happened. The police report concluded that the truck driver had caused the impact by pulling away from the curb, thereby striking the cyclist. I questioned the investigating officer and determined that not only had he not seen the accident, he'd never interviewed the bicycle rider, either. Incredibly enough, he had also neglected to interview the truck driver sufficiently, who spoke only broken English. Though the police officer wouldn't actually admit it, he had simply assumed the truck driver was at fault. He also volunteered that neither witness had seen the accident. I determined that the investigating officer, by virtue of the statement he'd given, would not hurt us with any testimony he would give. The officer had given the driver a ticket for failure to exercise due care to a pedestrian, and the deranged fellow on the bike was apparently incapable of showing up in court.

I got the case three months after the fact. Lopez was still driving for the insured. When I met him, I asked for his license, which he could not produce. I found out that his license had been suspended over another ticket he had received. He'd never shown up in court, neither for the previous ticket nor the current one. He'd also been picked up for driving with a suspended license and one of his buddies had bailed him out.

Amazingly enough, he never told the catering company about the accident. They didn't find out until three months later, when an attorney's lien was sent to them. I contacted both witnesses and took statements from them. Neither one could offer anything conclusive about what happened, including a CTA bus supervisor who had arrived at the scene five minutes after the accident had occurred. As mentioned, the cyclist had been incoherent even before the accident, and had made a habit of riding all over the north side of Chicago aimlessly, usually in clement weather. He suffered from brain damage caused by an unknown source, and in the accident, he had sustained a broken arm and a fractured collarbone. I couldn't discern any damage on the catering truck from the accident—it was pretty beat-up, with lots of dents and scratches. The bike had since been discarded, so we never got a chance to inspect it.

Eventually, Lopez quit his job and returned to Mexico. In a way, we had a Mexican standoff; neither participant could, or would, testify against each other. The witnesses had no value to speak of. We will never know what really happened, and in his effort to prove negligence against the driver, the attorney representing the cyclist was fighting an uphill battle.

The catering company, in utilizing marginal workers without stringently checking their driving records, had provided a Pandora's box for claims, which represented a classic dilemma for the insurance industry. From an underwriting standpoint, it is a question of whether you can justify the risk. Justification on a risk normally means charging enough to make it worthwhile from a financial perspective.

When Henry Ford invented the automobile, he surely had no idea the trouble they would cause in the future. I have witnessed incredible, amazing, truly jaw-dropping circumstances arise from the use and misuse of cars. It would be an interesting experiment to calculate how many man hours-- between insurance agents, adjusters, attorneys, doctors, mechanics and greedy citizens--are dedicated to negotiating about, and mending the wounds of those handy machines we drive.

CHAPTER 6: RENTAL WRECKS

The insanity surrounding automobiles is not confined to those who own them. The use of rental cars provides some even more absurd scenarios. One ridiculous story involves the driver of a Hertz rental vehicle who hit another vehicle and then fled from the scene. The driver who had been hit said the driver had been a woman, but couldn't give a good description of her.

Hertz hired me to investigate. I confronted the fellow who had rented the car and asked him some questions. "Did you let someone else use the vehicle? "Where do you work? Where were you at the time of the accident?" He answered that he had only

One set of keys, that he lived alone, and that he hadn't let anyone else operate the car. Then he implied that someone had written the plate number down incorrectly. I told him frankly that we were quite sure that it was the car he had rented that had been involved in the accident __ it had damage on the left front fender. The man replied that the damage had happened in a parking lot at a shopping mall, and he hadn't made a police report. He didn't know at the time that we had a positive paint transfer on the car he, or someone, had hit.

A few days after I interviewed him, the man called the rental company and admitted that he'd been the driver. He chose not to reveal any details. Hertz had no language in their rental contract about denying coverage for such an odd situation, so they went ahead and paid the claim. If the exposure had been larger, the company might have thought twice about a client who had fled the scene of an accident without filing a police report; but since it was a fender bender, they paid the claim, avoiding having to pay lawyers an even greater amount.

This scenario was nothing compared to what I'd come across in my career.

The Fallacious Valet

I have done some work for a rental car company. The fellow from whom I received my first case was named Tom Lauper. The pop singer Cindy Lauper was popular back then, so his name was easy to remember. He also happened to be a heck of a nice guy, and very shrewd to boot. He didn't know it at the time, but he got me started on a great run with a great company. He left a year or so after I received my first case.

It all began when I called his company one day and told him that I had experience in handling rental car cases. I said I believed I would be an asset to them. After the conversation, I forgot all about it for a while, though I sent him some material regarding my company, which he didn't pitch in the garbage like a lot of people do. A month and a half later, I was thrilled when he called and gave me a case, sight unseen. Immediately, I developed a fine reputation as I was able to sort out this complex mess of a case that he'd given me. He spread the word before he left, and his co-workers, a couple of ladies with New York accents, started giving me work.

The case involved Brandon Sloan, who had rented a car and was going to a near north-side restaurant with his girlfriend. Sloan, who was from out of town, was in Chicago on business. At the restaurant, he gave the car to a valet parking service. The valet, who wasn't identified until much later, took the wheel, tried to make a U-turn illegally, and hit a woman on a motor scooter, breaking her leg. When questioned by the police, the valet gave a false name, and the police inexplicably never asked him for his driver's license.

At first, I figured the valet, having given his name as Johnny Stines, must have known the real Johnny Stines, because the valet gave a good address, but a bogus phone number and a partially accurate date of birth, with the correct day and month, but the wrong year. The one fundamental difference was that the valet was Hispanic, and the guy he fingered as the driver was black. It was obvious we were dealing with a real professional con artist. I found out later that Johnny Stines, the fellow who was implicated as the driver, had lost his driver's license and someone else was using it. I tried to find this fellow, Stines, so I traveled to his southside home. His mother, being the God-fearing and honest person that she was, told me where I could find him. I interviewed him at work and took his picture, because we wanted to show it was not the man who had been driving the car. We wanted to demonstrate that we were dealing with a phony.

He was working at a near north-side parking garage as an attendant, and he was unassuming and forthright. After asking him a series of questions, I found out that his wallet had been stolen, or he'd lost it, and he'd been forced to obtain a duplicate driver's license. His employer liked him enough to cooperate and gave me his time cards to prove that he'd been working at the garage at the time he'd been allegedly driving the rental car for the valet parking service.

The valet parking service had no insurance, or so they claimed. Pinning them down was like wrestling with a greased pig. They flat-out refused to identify who the driver had been who had assumed Stines name. My goal was to get the valet parking service to take the matter over themselves. After all, they had been in control of the car, and they were profiting from the concession for the restaurant. They were, in fact, responsible. It finally turned out that they did have liability coverage with a good company, but they had a $10,000 deductible for property damage and bodily injury.

Before this fact was made known, we insisted that the attorney representing the injured party produce her for a statement. They did so. I had photos of the real Johnny Stines, and she told me, unequivocally, it was not him. I wasn't surprised. Before the interview, I didn't know the actual driver was Hispanic, but the injured party described him as a dark complected fellow of Hispanic origin.

Suit was filed against the rental car company and the driver. The rental car company hired an attorney who was running on five cylinders with an eight-cylinder engine. The process of discovery began, and the attorneys for the rental car company eventually brought the valet parking service into the suit by virtue of a third party action. I made at least 30 phone calls to the valet parking service to identify the driver, and I went out on a Friday night to find the owner. They did their best to avoid me, and I didn't even have a subpoena.

When I interviewed the renter of the car, Sloan and his girl-friend told me that the fellow who had taken possession of the car at the restaurant appeared to have some kind of an accent, perhaps Jamaican, and they described him as being black. They wanted the valet parking service to accept full responsibility. They still had the ticket that they'd been handed when they'd relinquished possession of the car. But the rental car company was trying to stick Sloan with a bill for the damage caused to the rental car as a result of the accident. For some reason, his credit card didn't provide him with the insurance coverage to satisfy that obligation.

This case had a value ranging from $60,000 to $90,000. The injured party had a compound fracture where the bone had broken through the skin, which had required an open reduction procedure.

Cases in Cook County don't come to trial very expeditiously. Five years later, the same defense attorney was still on the case for the rental car company. They should have fired him. This attorney had an investigator trying to find the real Johnny Stines; they tracked him down to the Robert Taylor homes, a housing project complex for the indigent. He had moved a couple of times since I had met him. The rental car company had already been dismissed from the case, and what was needed was an affidavit signed by the real Johnny Stines, stating that he hadn't been the valet that night, and that it was a case of someone using his name fraudulently. I would not call it a case of mistaken identity, because the valet had deliberately and falsely given the police another man's name. When I inter-viewed the investigating officer, who soon realized that I thought he was a dope for not following proper procedure in requiring the valet to produce a valid driver's license, he abruptly aborted the interview. He would not allow me to tape the interview, either, which was unfortunate because I really had him on the defensive. Maybe the valet had paid him off, slipping him 50 bucks to look the other way. Even with so many people around, nobody ever came forward to say they'd seen any exchange of money.

If someone could secure an affidavit, the rental car company would no longer have any obligation to defend or indemnify any-one for the accident. The rental car company and the renter would be free and clear from the burden of the lawsuit. I got a call from the rental car company asking if I could get it done. My first reaction was to admonish them for calling me off the case after I'd done my initial investigation, but I kept my mouth from flapping.

The affidavit prepared by the attorney had some misspellings and improper wording, which I corrected. Now 1 had to figure out a way to get this guy, Johnny Stines, to sign it ___ he had no phone and he wasn't working any longer. I wrote him a letter, but he didn't respond, so I decided to go to the Robert Taylor homes in early February, at 8:00 a.m., when it was 10 degrees outside. The Chicago Housing Authority (CHA) has a police department in an adjacent building, as the Robert Taylor Homes are high-rise hell holes. A cave would provide safer and more luxurious accommodations. Not withstanding the crime, the cockroaches, the filth, the excrement, urine, and dried-up chicken wings made visiting the place a virtual nightmare.

1 parked my car and ran into the building close to the police station to avoid being shot or knifed. The people inside looked as if they'd seen a ghost. I asked for the chief, and while I never learned whether he was the chief or

the assistant, the man who greeted me was gracious enough to talk to me. I told him why 1 was there. "So what?" he retorted. "What do you want me to do about it?" I asked him for an escort up to the 14th floor. At first he said no, but I guess I looked pretty determined. I replied, "I'm going up there anyway, then. Will you consider the bad publicity if a white guy from the suburbs gets killed on your turf?"

He thought about it for a few seconds and said, "You're right." He sent me up with two armed policemen, and as I was departing, he said, "You're walking because the elevators are broken"

Unfortunately, my guy wasn't home. He was out visiting an auntie or a girlfriend, according to his mother. She said he would definitely be home on Thursday, though. That was two days away. Some 48 hours later, I barged into the CHA Police Department again. This time, I didn't have to ask for the chief. He looked quite exasperated because I was back, and it seemed as if it was on the tip of his tongue to tell me to get lost. Without my having to ask, he sent two policemen, who walked up with me the 14 flights of stairs. Johnny Stines was there and recognized me. I sent the policemen on their way, and the surprised affidavit-signer got out of bed and put on his clothes. Stines' brother was there, too. I had a trench coat on with lapels and a belt, along with a Kangol hat that some golfers wear. He told me I looked like Inspector Clouseau. We walked back down the stairs without incident, and I took him to the currency exchange at 47th and King Drive, where we had the affidavit signed and notarized. I paid him $20 for his trouble and he was appreciative.

The affidavit took the rental car company out of the case for good, though the judge had already let them out via summary judgment. Now that the alleged driver of the rental car, Stines, was dropped as a defendant in the case, the rental car company no longer had a fiduciary responsibility to defend anyone in the case. It was a great victory for the rental car company because the exposure to the injured party was extinguished, and it stopped the meter regarding the defense attorney's fee. I charged them $950 for my efforts and they were happy to pay it. I never went back to the Robert Taylor Homes, and I hope I never will.

In the end, the valet parking service paid the entire claim, and rightfully so.

The Inside Job

Major car rental companies need to be extremely vigilant about security because of the nature of their workforce. A lot of people working on the lower spectrum of the pay scale have the attitude that with their extensive education and finely honed job skills, the world owes them a living. It is a fact of life, but you have to watch your employees and put in systems to combat theft and other problems.

I was getting a bunch of claims involving stolen rental cars at one point. A car would be stolen, involved in a hit-and- run accident, and sometimes an unauthorized driver would flee from the scene of the accident on foot. Typically, these accidents happened in the city, in a high-crime neighborhood. I would investigate the claims and contact the uninsured motorist carrier for the person or persons making injury claims against the rental car company. Usually, I would turn the matter over to them. We were successful almost 100 percent of the time because under Illinois law (and the same is true of most other states), no coverage is mandated when a vehicle is driven by an unauthorized driver, or if the vehicle is in a state of theft. The person driving the rental car would technically be uninsured because he or she is not authorized to operate that car. That premise would open the door to tap into the uninsured motorist coverage, a first- party coverage, applying to the injured party through his or her automobile carrier. On behalf of the rental car company, I would send out denial letters to the injured party or their attorneys, informing them that coverage was not being provided for any third-party injury claims.

This letter would trigger the opening of a file with the uninsured motorist carrier. Insurance companies are very careful in handling uninsured motorist claims because it is a first-party coverage, meaning the insured is making a claim against his own insurance company. The courts have little patience for insurance companies that play games with their own policy holders. This is a pure contractual relationship that is held sacred by the courts. A third-party claimant has no contractual relationship with the insurance carrier with whom the claim is being made. The courts are much less stringent and protective when it comes to third-party claims.

Substandards have a deserved reputation for not paying third-party claims until they have to, or are forced to, vis-a-vis a judgment. However, almost all substandards honor their contractual obligations to their insured, including collision or comprehensive losses or medical pay claims. Most run a tight ship, and rarely do they overpay claims on a first- or third- party basis.

They have lots of ways to restrict their cash outlays, such as using captive body shops, which are shops that don't normally use original manufactured car parts, known as OEM parts. Also, they use severe restrictions regarding medical pay outlays by inserting language in the policy saying that they will pay medical bills if there is no other coverage available to the insured. They also are famous for utilizing named driver exclusions for certain people in a household designating the children or spouse won't be covered. Standard companies don't follow these types of practices as a rule. They charge more, but there are fewer loopholes.

One of the claims I handled gave me some good insight into how serious this problem with employee theft at car rental companies had become. An employee at a well-known outfit figured out how to print rental agreements so as to allow accomplices to remove cars from the rental car hubs without anyone suspecting a problem. This person knew how to manipulate the computer and programs that were being used to devise rental agreements. At least 40 cars turned up missing in a 45-day period. That was almost a car a day! When you have a fleet of 13 to 14,000 cars, sometimes more than a couple of cars missing will not be discovered right away.

Several of these 40 cars were eventually involved in accidents. I would investigate, and ultimately deny any claims that were forthcoming. Some of the attorneys for the injured par-ties maintained that the rental car company was culpable for these accidents, even though there had been an unauthorized driver—they cited a breach of security. There is no case law supporting that theory yet, but someday it may be tested. If the appellate court ruled that there is merit with this breach of security allegation, then maybe the rental car companies would have to step up security or pay the piper.

No doubt, several of these cases were fascinating because of the ingenious methods of fraud. A lady from Melrose Park was involved in an accident with a couple of people in Maywood. One of the drivers had no coverage at all and never came for-ward; the woman had coverage with a substandard. I denied her injury claim and their subsequent property damage subrogation claim as well. The carrier tried to get the couple's money back from us.

The rental car driver had run a red light, causing a three-car collision. I went to the police station in Maywood to secure the police report, and along with that, they gave me the rental agreement. The police officer had evidently pulled the rental agreement out of the glove box of the rental car. What a stroke of luck, especially considering that the police officer had no idea that the rental car was stolen. It was a great gesture on his part to provide us with the document, even though he did not know of its significance. I called my local contact and ascertained that the arbitrary number assigned to the car was phony. Each car has a number assigned to it, and this one was not correct it applied to a completely different car. The rental car company could not figure out why so many cars were missing, but at that point, I figured it out. The rental agreement I had was a poor copy, so I had my contact run a better one. He immediately recognized the discrepancy.

I called the driver and arranged an interview with a translator as she did not speak much English. She said that she had borrowed the car from a neighbor who, of course, was no longer here. He was back in Mexico. She had no idea the car was illegitimately rented. The driver, to top it off, did not possess a legitimate driver's license, but she did have a permit.

She had used the car to go to her doctor's office to have a D & C, and was on her way back home when the accident occurred.

It just so happened that her cousin, who lived down the block, worked in reservations at the rental car company. We were able to successfully prove, without having to defend any lawsuits, by virtue of sending letters and documents to the injured party's attorney and to her carrier, that the rental car was in a state of theft. At first blush, the feeling by the carrier was that we were trying to walk away from something that we had a duty to pay. Their paranoia stemmed from the outrageousness of their own practices and tactics. We proved that the rental agreement was a phony, and that the driver was unauthorized. I talked at length to their in-house counsel about it, and he convinced the claim department that filing suit would not result in any type of judgment against my principal, the rental car company. I saved the rental car company at least $10,000 in legal fees by being so per-suasive, once they realized that we were telling the truth. Subsequently, they backed off.

This particular company wrote the book on denying claims because of an unauthorized driver exclusion triggered by an unauthorized driver operating one of their insured vehicles. A denial would not be based on liability issues, but on the fact that no coverage would be afforded to an unauthorized driver. Local management at the rental car company wanted to be kept abreast of what I found out, and in the end, three people were identified and terminated. The phony rental caper stopped. They also put blocks in the computer to prevent it from happening again. Nobody ever

called to thank me, which I didn't expect, but I was paid well and the work
kept coming.

Just Who's Behind the Wheel?

Another case involving an accident in a stolen rental car was notable because
the passenger in the car suffered brain damage. **On** the southside, near the
lake, he hit the windshield with a thunderous blow. He'd also been under the
impression that the driver of the rental car had been in possession of the
vehicle legally. In fact, the car had been missing for more than three weeks,
and was not discovered until the Chicago Police ran the registration after the
accident and called the rental car company. The vehicle had been stolen from
one of the main hubs, most likely by an employee with an accomplice.

It was a bad accident with multiple injuries, but the passenger received
the worst of it--he had more than $75,000 in medical bills. His attorney let
me interview him, even though I told the attorney up front that we probably
wouldn't be able to do anything from a coverage standpoint. The driver of the
car was never found--he'd given a bogus name to the police. The passenger
knew him only as a classmate at a vocational school for adults on the
southside of Chicago.

The passenger did not tell a very convincing story about how they'd met
up the day of the accident, though. According to his story, he'd been waiting
at a bus stop three or four miles from the scene of the accident. The driver
had seen him and offered him a ride. Allegedly, they had planned to visit a
mutual friend when the driver ran a red light and was hit by a truck. Four
different vehicles were involved. The passenger was taken to Michael Reese
Hospital, and the driver was taken to Northwestern Memorial.

The police who handled the case had gone to Northwestern Memorial to
question the driver about his possession of the vehicle and what had
transpired in the accident. When interviewed, the paramedics reported that
the guy had a possible punctured lung, broken ribs, and a laceration on his
forehead that would probably require 35 to 40 stitches. Neither occupant in
the rental car had been wearing a seatbelt. When the police arrived at the
hospital, though, the driver was gone. He had been connected to an IV in an
emergency room cubicle, and he'd simply walked out of the hospital before
the police arrived. He was never found.

In the end, as I predicted, all claims were denied. I took a statement from the police officer on the case, and he stated that he had never talked to the driver. He did say he'd called the rental car company because he'd had a strong suspicion that the rental car was stolen. At the rental company, he'd spoken to someone who told him that the vehicle in question was not, in fact, missing or considered stolen. I asked who exactly he had spoken to, but he hadn't taken down the name. He couldn't even remember the number he'd called.

The computerized record of movement showed that the vehicle had been unaccounted for at least two and a half to three weeks, but the company didn't know it was missing until the day of the accident. I had one of the managers file a stolen vehicle report, post-accident. The last time the vehicle had been rented out had been three weeks before the accident, and it had been returned the next day.

The injured passenger said he had seen the driver operate this vehicle before the accident. Furthermore, he related that the driver had been in possession of the vehicle for at least a couple of months prior to the accident! I did some checking, and there was no evidence we could find to support this allegation. It occurred to me that the driver may have had another vehicle like it that may have also have been stolen.

After we denied the passenger's claim, the attorney filed suit, alleging that the rental car company was culpable because of lack of security. The case was ultimately dismissed without prejudice, which means that the plaintiff attorney had a year to reinstate the case. The defense attorney could not convince the judge to grant a summary judgment. The passenger, through his attorney, never had the case reinstated. The passenger tried to garner our sympathy, or at least empathy, but we were not buying into that at all. He'd never had ownership of a vehicle, and thus he had no uninsured motorist coverage to fall back on. When you get close to the fire, I guess, sometimes you get burned.

Slick Operators

I also had a couple of rental car cases where someone's credit card was stolen. In one instance, the card was used to rent a car. It made me wonder just how carefully driver's licenses were being checked. In addition, purchases were made to the tune of more than $10,000. The thieves had used the card to establish credit, and had used it to take more than $7,500 in merchandise from various stores. It all happened within a 48- hour period.

In another instance, someone had taken a number off of a credit card and had used it to rent a car. Of course, the vehicle was involved in an accident. It was never explained satisfactorily how this could physically be possible. When the victim of such theft cooperates, we will talk to them in an effort to demonstrate that they are not the perpetrator of fraud, and we will deny any claims that might come forward because of any accident.

There are some really slick operators out there with vulture-like tendencies, though. I once identified a driver in a similar scenario. I knew she had a vehicle without permission or through a legitimate rental. I arranged a meeting with her to try and find out what her story was, but she refused to meet with me. I called and left a message for **her** stating that if she didn't cooperate, she could explain her story to the State Attorney's Office. Then I followed up with a letter pointing the facts out succinctly, but she still would not communicate with me. I called the State Attorney's Office and the Chicago Police, but they wouldn't touch it. That refusal shows you how overburdened our justice system is.

The Ugliest of the Ugly

The most bizarre case was one involving a chef and apartment building owner. This fellow was in a dance club when another patron bumped into him, apologizing profusely. He thought nothing of it until later in the evening, when he realized his wallet was gone. The thief had gotten everything, including his driver's license, social security card, and a couple of documents showing his bank account information. He notified his bank the next morning. They said they would watch his account, and that it wasn't necessary to actually close the account.

The man owned a multi-unit building, and he put rent money in a special account to keep his records straight. About a month later, though, a deposit was made into his account comprised of stolen personal checks from a woman in the southern suburbs of the city. The next day, $13,000 was withdrawn. Fortunately, I was able to get my hands on a video of an African-American man in the act of making the transaction. The only problem was that the true owner of the card, Pierre Pilotte, was Caucasian. The bank eventually admitted their error, but waited 90 days to replace the cash. I agreed with Mr. Pilotte that the account should have been closed immediately.

While the true Pierre was counting on the bank to protect him, the fictitious Pierre Pilotte had befriended a fellow in the South Shore neighborhood, and Mr. Fictitious was allowed by this friend to use his legitimately rented car to run a quick errand. That night, an accident occurred: the thief struck a car being driven by a model, who jammed her wrist on the steering wheel, resulting in carpal tunnel syndrome that ultimately required surgery.

The rental car wasn't appreciably damaged, but the model's car was. The impostor actually stayed at the scene of the accident and presented his driver's license to the police. He had taken the license from the real Pierre Pilotte and had inserted his own picture onto it! The police had no clue. He was ticketed, and he never showed up for court. A warrant was issued for his arrest. The guy who rented the car had no idea that the fellow that was driving the rental car out to run a quick errand was a shyster. I met this legitimate renter and took his photograph. He was definitely a victim of a scam as well as the real Pierre Pilotte. He did not match up to the photograph of the fellow that was in the bank. The real Pierre Pilotte had to do a lot of explaining and backtracking.

I wrote a letter on his behalf explaining to his bank that he was trustworthy and had not been involved in the rental car scandal. He also used the letter to show the police that he was innocent and undeserving of arrest. We were able to show conclusively that the driver of the car had taken the vehicle under false pretenses. The aspiring actress and model who had been injured went through her own carrier, making an uninsured motorist claim.

The fictitious Pierre Pilotte was never found. He supposedly lived in New York City; we had a phone number for him that was unpublished and eventually disconnected, but we never did have an address for him. As the story unfolded, I learned that the renter's brother had befriended the errant driver, and had actually spent a lot of time with him before they became comfortable enough to allow him to use one of their cars.

Another wild story about a rental car involves a fellow whose son was in a gang. Eventually, the boy was killed in gang war-fare. The man, an accountant, had a rental car and was living on the southside of Chicago. He happened to be on his way to see a client when he was accosted and attacked, while in the car, at a stop light at 67th and State Street. Forced to stay in the car, he was taken to a house and kept under guard for four days, unallowed to leave. His wife had no idea where he'd gone. In the meantime, the car was involved in a hit-and-run accident. The gang let him go after four days, and even returned the car, with damage. Unwilling to tell the real story, he explained to the rental company that he had bumped another car in traffic. They didn't seem to be troubled about the minor cosmetic damage. Elsewhere, a claim was made by the victim of the hit-and-run.

When the gang members who kidnapped him let him go, they told him they would kill one of his sons, who happened to be 18 years of age, if he told anyone, including the police, what had really occurred. They also extorted money from him to add to his grief. When I finally tracked him down, he was living in Columbus, Ohio. I finally persuaded him to tell his story, but it took a month of prodding to get him to talk. He was scared out of his mind. I concluded that his story had a ring of truth to it; it was so preposterous that the effort to make it up to avoid dealing with a $10,000 claim wasn't worth it!

The claim, however, was denied by the rental car company, and his insurance company, which was primary, also denied it. The injured party fell back on their uninsured motorist coverage for satisfaction and payment of the injury claims. Our renter never filed a stolen car report with the Chicago Police for fear of severe retribution. We've all heard about the witness protection program; this fellow and his family needed a new identity, and quick.

Low Impact, High Drama

Several rental car companies operated, and continue to operate, at Chicago's number-two airport. At that time, there were multiple car hikers taking rental cars back and forth from the rental offices to the airport. That set-up is no longer employed at Midway Airport. A couple of employees from one company had a low-speed accident in the parking area for rental cars about a thousand feet from the terminals. The parking lot was so congested that going five miles per hour would have been the top possible speed. Both of the injured workers made a claim against the other company. I checked it out and deter-mined that our driver, who was alone, had been in the striking vehicle. The other driver was almost equally at fault for not keeping a proper lookout, but not quite.

The passenger working for the other company made a workers' compensation claim and hired an attorney so that her case didn't get settled right away. It took about a year to get all the bills and records regarding her case. It was hard to imagine that either party, driver or passenger, had been injured. The damage on the rental car with the two occupants had run a little over $1,200, and it doesn't take much of an impact to cause that amount of damage, particularly with all the lightweight materials used in manufacturing vehicles today.

Two months after the accident, I settled the claim of the driver of the second rental car. He was not represented by an attorney. He had a bill from the Cook County Hospital for emergency room treatment for over $600, where he'd had some x-rays. He'd also had one follow-up visit to his company doctor, as his employer demanded a check-up before he would be allowed to return to work. That was the extent of his medical attention. Though he complained of neck and back pain, he was off work for just three days.

This man was a stout individual, not quite 30 years old. I gave him $1,600, and he was responsible for paying the bills out of the settlement proceeds. When I delivered the check to him and had him sign the release form, he said he felt fine with no residual soreness, stiffness, or physical complications from the accident. He signed a release of all claims, along with an addendum saying he would cooperate in securing a dollar contract through the Industrial Commission. I had added that purposely to further protect the rental car company. The workers' compensation statute is three years in Illinois, and the statute of limitations is two years for bodily injury. I never thought I would hear from him again.

A year and a half later, I received an attorney's lien from a well-known personal injury attorney practicing law in downtown Chicago. I called the attorney handling the case and learned the fellow I had settled with had serious lower back problems, which he was trying to relate to this low-speed accident. The attorney told me I hadn't given him enough consideration (better known as money) for his injury. My first reaction was to laugh. I had only seen one other attempt to break a release, and it had been unsuccessful. I told the attorney that the consideration given was commensurate with the facts of the case, including what was known about the injury at the time. I further emphasized to the attorney that we are not mind readers, or able to peer into the future. Additionally, I indicated that the language in the release was such that it was almost impossible to break unless fraud was involved.

I had a very incisive conversation with the attorney about the merits of the case. In the course of our discussion, 1 found out that his client had already had back surgery and his bills were over $33,000. The surgery had been performed almost a year and eight months after the accident had occurred. The attorney told me he thought he had a good chance to break the release, especially because the statute had not expired yet. He also said that he felt it was worth the effort __________ if they could overturn the release of all claims, he thought he could get a judgment of well over $150,000. I pointed out that his client had been the driver, and was guilty of significant comparative fault based on Illinois law. I also pointed out that it hadn't been much of an impact.

The car rental company hired a very shrewd attorney who did the necessary research and cited the voluminous case law in Illinois about trying to challenge a release of all claims. The conclusion was that unless fraud was involved, and improper consideration was given, the courts would uphold the sanctity of the release form practically 100 percent of the time. The other side argued that we had taken advantage of this poor man by giving him over $900 above and beyond his hospital bill.

Suit was filed, and the case went on for about six months with both attorneys preparing briefs and making motions. The judge who heard the case said the release itself was quite powerful, but the fact that the injured party signed the addendum saying he would cooperate with us in securing a dollar contract through the Industrial Commission suggested that the injured party believed in his own mind, at the time that he had signed the release and addendum, that he was physically okay. The judge ruled, saying that the release of all claims would stand, and couldn't be broken or overturned.

The lawyer for the injured party talked to me about three months later, saying that it was definitely worth a try to pursue it, though he had no stomach to appear before the appellate court. I'm quite sure the rental car company would have appealed had they lost in the first round. This case, among others, put me on very solid ground with the rental car company.

A couple of days after we learned who had won the release challenge, I received $28,000 from the state of Nebraska, who monitored insurance companies going into receivership. It was amazing that after six years, we were able to recover almost 60 cents on the dollar regarding a settlement that we had made on an uninsured motorist exposure. This was because the insolvent insurance company could not meet their obligations and responsibilities. Most states have a guarantee fund in which all companies doing business in that state make contributions. The fund was created so that there would be money if and when these situations occurred. Another feather in the cap.

The Best Defense is a Good Offense

Envision a 90-year-old woman, maybe your mother or grandmother, walking the streets of the north side of Chicago, in a reasonably safe neighborhood, on a positively balmy January evening—it was approximately 50 degrees. Granny had dark clothes on; though it wasn't raining, there was a light drizzle.

The manager for a rental car company was driving a company car home. He didn't see her when he was making a left turn, and he hit her while she was in the crosswalk. Clearly, he was obliged to yield to the elderly woman, since he was making a turn on a green light. Furthermore, she was actually walking toward him rather than away from him. Granny suffered multiple fractures. She must have been a tough old bird, because after extensive rehab, I'm happy to say she made a nice recovery.

Being, by all accounts, a very sharp and independent woman, Granny hired an attorney to go after both the driver and his company, which was involved despite the fact that the driver was going home. The driver had made a few stops before coming home from his office- all were business-related. The attorney, who shall remain nameless, was one of the most unscrupulous people I have ever dealt with. In my view, he should have been disbarred long before I had the displeasure of doing business with him. He was, however, a great advocate for his client. He just went way over the line, and he didn't do it in a particularly clever way, either: he actually told a witness that if she didn't affirm his client's story, she would be in "big trouble," which intimidated her. This witness had experienced a stroke a couple of months prior to his admonition, and she couldn't remember everything in much detail. The truth is, she wouldn't have been a factor in the case because of her memory loss, so the attorney had no need to threaten her.

I had a very difficult time finding this lady, but eventually, after knocking on a lot of doors, I found out that she was living in a nursing home. By that time, I had also learned the identities of a couple of other witnesses who claimed to have seen the accident, but they were not listed on the police report. These folks were alleging that the headlight on the rental company car had been out, meaning that the attorney could keep the rental car company in the case. If there were some type of defect in the rental car, which could be proven, the attorney would be assured that his client would have two targets: the driver and the rental car company.

Illinois is a non-vicarious state, meaning that the negligence of a renter/driver cannot be imputed to the rental car company. The rental car company caps their responsibility in these situations by providing liability coverage for the renter/driver. In some cases these limits set forth are the mini-mum limits mandated by the state in the car rental statute. The company employee had the benefit of more coverage than the average renter. If the renter/driver desires more coverage, they can purchase it at the time when they rent the vehicle or they can look to their own carrier. Typically, in an auto accident, the rental car company would be dismissed from the case, and thus the rental car company would have to defend the driver.

The witnesses were clearly shills. I couldn't find anyone else to affirm that the left front headlight had been out on the company car, nor did the rental car company keep a record of replacing headlights or other bulbs. No photographs had been taken at the scene of the accident. A lady in a tavern on the northwest corner of the intersection who had been working as a bartender confirmed that the car had hit the lady—she knew nothing about any head-light being out. There were other witnesses listed in the discovery process who had been thrown into the mix by the plaintiff attorney with the purpose of obfuscating the issue. 1 tracked each and every one of them down, and none could confirm the question of the headlight. None had seen much of the impact either. Lastly, 1 tracked down the investigating officer, who didn't remember any-thing about a headlight. The only witness the officer knew was the bartender. It soon became apparent that the woman in the nursing home had been a shill from the beginning. She'd gotten religion after her stroke.

I guess I was stirring up too much controversy by contacting all the people put forth as star witnesses by the plaintiff's attorney—a man by the name of Goldmeier---so he decided to depose me, too. I'm sure he was getting an earful from his witnesses about me asking a lot of embarrassing questions. I decided to consult with the defense attorney, who was present when I was deposed. The plaintiff attorney was an admittedly ornery sort, and I became very testy and contentious when the attorney tried to discredit my efforts in the case by asking how much I'd been paid by the rental car company, and what volume of work I received from them. He was trying to show prejudice on my part. He also asked all sorts of personal questions about my level of education and my insurance background. I simply refused to answer the majority of his questions, and every time I did so, he would screech, "You refuse to answer questions propounded by the court?!"

I answered, "I refuse to answer your questions, which are irrelevant!" This son of a gun was trying to demonstrate that I was a captive investigator, hired by the car rental company to change the facts of the case. Because I refused to answer the majority of his questions, the tension was palpable. My sneer certainly didn't help matters.

After we were done, I commented to the defense attorney that he ought to lodge a complaint with the bar association for unethical behavior on the part of this attorney for threatening a witness. The defense attorney didn't think it was a good idea. It was patently clear that the shyster attorney was trying to cover up his own malfeasance by making me look like the bad guy, which was okay with me, to a point. I just wasn't willing to go along with his entire charade, and I had made a bit of a mockery of his attempt to deflect attention from his own unscrupulous behavior.

When the deposition took place, a year and a half had passed since the accident. The injured granny had made a decent recovery, which was remarkable for a 90-year-old. The case settled for $200,000.

Later, I heard that the manager of the rental car company in the claim department was unhappy that the defense attorney was not able to achieve a better result. The claimant had $60,000 in bills that needed to be paid out of the settlement, and she'd had multiple fractures. To me $200,000 sounded reasonable, but maybe a little on the high side. Liability was not much of an issue, because the driver should have seen her before it was too late.

Ostensibly, this elderly woman could have lived to the age of 105! She didn't have any close family, so there were no heirs to carry on her case if she died. Sometimes when a person gets old, their lives become an afterthought from a "value" standpoint, especially when they don't have any close family. My assumption is that there was a feeling that the case could have been settled for significantly less because of that sad fact.

I had to go back to the nearby bar on another case about a year and a half after the case involving the elderly woman had settled, and I met up with one of the bartenders I had interviewed as a witness. We got to talking, and she said that our granny claimant was still out walking in semi-inclement weather, and had almost been hit again. The only concession she'd made to the fact that she'd had a bad accident was the cane she sported.

Structural Work Act

One contractor's negligence may be instrumental in causing another contractor's employee to get hurt on a job. The State of Illinois no longer has on its books a unique statute called by many the Scaffolding Act. Its true name is the Structural Work Act. An interesting case I was involved with did not meet the standard of the Structural Work Act or the proper criterion. A similar case, on the other hand, was a classic example falling under the purview of the act. It was an unusual circumstance involving illegal aliens. The discussion of this scenario merits recounting a third case.

The first case centered around a custodian who was cleaning out an apartment for a landlord. He was an independent contractor—the landlord was paying him in cash. He had no workers' compensation coverage for himself. The landlord had no such coverage either, and when the custodian became injured, he sued the landlord for what we call in the business a "latent defect."

When the custodian had made the seemingly foolish decision to dump a five- gallon bucket of water over the railing of the third-floor back porch, the momentum had carried him crashing into the railing, which had then splintered and broken away on one side. The 240-pound man dropped to the alley below and sustained severe, but not life-threatening injuries, including five fractured ribs, a broken leg, and a shattered left ankle. As soon as he was physically capable, he immediately hired counsel. I never got the opportunity to talk to him at all.

I found out that the railing's wood had been rotten, and the insured claimed he'd been unaware of that fact. The insured said that he had intended to overhaul the porch system the following summer. Because the insured didn't know about the problem, the injured party had not had the benefit of fair warning. In my eyes, it appeared to be a case to settle. The injured party was a neighborhood handyman, who had never worked for the insured before the accident. The accident had been very serious, but given the facts, it certainly did not fall under the purview of the Structural Work Act because the work being done had not involved any construction or alterations to the building. The Structural Work Act mandates that no negligence can be assigned to the injured party, therefore making it almost impossible for the injured party not to collect from some culpable party. The responsible party could be an owner of a piece of property or a building, a general contractor, or an architect, developer or a sub-contractor from the job.

As has happened with all too many of my cases, I never did find out what happened to the poor guy who fell. I knew that the carrier was highly irritated, however.

I was, in fact, instructed not to take any statements from people who might prove the case for the injured party, which is standard advice. Instead, I provided verbal reports which eliminated the need to send them written reports for fear my reports could be subpoenaed by the other side at some point. Nevertheless, the carrier was feeling very edgy. I wanted to tell them that they couldn't have it both ways, but I didn't. While I felt that they needed to know what they were up against without putting it in writing, I also got the sense that the file handler was mistrustful of my verbal reportage. Perhaps they were afraid that a trail would be left for the plaintiff to pounce on, which would force them to ante up and make a bona fide attempt to settle the claim.

Another similar case involved what I called the Flying Wallendas. A Polish contractor had been doing work for a company that advertised on late-night television the installation of house siding that would never need repainting. The company had hired a bunch of small contractors, with four or five seasonal workers to install the siding and also to do gutter work and some roofing jobs. The general contractor was not a proponent of close supervision. Essentially, the subcontractor was told where the jobs were, and the workers would show up after getting the materials from the general contractor. The subcontractor had no insurance for its employees, and there was no formal contract between the general contractor and the subcontractor.

On one such job, the Polish subcontractor doing the work put scaffolding up three stories high on a frame building on the north-west side of Chicago. Someone from the general contractor's office dropped by the building, saw the scaffolding, and made no objections. Shortly thereafter, two workers fell 40 feet to the ground when the scaffolding collapsed. One Polish worker died, and his coworker ended up paralyzed from the waist down, with multiple fractures all over his body. A neighbor had heard the scaffolding creak just 30 seconds before it had collapsed.

As noted above, any agreement the two contractors had was verbal in nature. There were no written documents save some primitive invoices that had been sent as work was completed. To complicate things further, both injured workers were illegal aliens. Luckily for them, they still received protection under U.S. law. The one fellow who had survived had his own cause of action; the family of the deceased brought an action on behalf of their relative. The fact that the two workers who had fallen had been instrumental in setting up the rickety scaffolding had no bearing whatsoever on the case. Their own stark and obvious negligence could not be used to mitigate their claims. Rather, the general contractor's carrier paid the freight on the case.

The third case may bear an explanation. It was not a Structural Work Case because the Structural Work Act had been abolished by the Tort Reform Act of 1995 in the State of Illinois. Even today, the courts still follow the old doctrine that people in charge of construction projects are responsible for safety on the job. I believe this is rooted in the fact that the general contractor or owner has the authority to shut down a work site if and when there are unsafe conditions. Rarely have I heard of this happening before a tragic accident, however---usually, it happens after a tragic accident. A case in point was the construction of a new ballpark in Milwaukee.

A general contractor, wearing a second hat as a developer, was building a one- story office building in the western suburbs of Chicago. He relied a great deal on a carpentry subcontractor to do a major part of the construction work. This subcontractor had a very bright foreman on the job. Most of the workers on the job were regulars, having been with the company for at least a couple of years. When a man was injured on the site, breaking his neck, he was considered a marginal worker. At the time of the accident, he had been working side by side with another fellow hanging trusses. The unlucky worker had nailed a truss in four places, the truss weighing between 200 and 300 pounds. While cutting through one of the nails holding the truss up with a power saw, he had inadvertently been resting his full weight on that very truss. When it collapsed, he had fallen, landing on a concrete curb ten feet below. He'd hit the curb like a missile, crashing squarely on his hard hat. Immediately, he lost all movement.

In the days that followed, his co-worker refused to talk to me. They had been good friends, and I suspect that he didn't want to admit that he should have warned his friend, or that his friend had made a foolish move. Since they hadn't been under orders to work at a breakneck speed, they clearly should have nailed the truss more securely before cutting or putting weight on it. Industry norm in the carpentry trades indicates a safer method of fastening trusses before trimming them. Incidentally, I never had a chance to interview him, either.

The carrier who had hired me wrote an additional insured endorsement, which named the general contractor as a co-insured party on the carpentry subcontractor's liability policy. We in the business call it an additional insured. The subcontractor's carrier defends the general contractor for any claims brought against the general contractor by an employee of the subcontractor, or by an act of negligence from one the employees of that subcontractor, resulting in injury or property damage to anyone on that job or project. This is a means of shifting responsibility for the payment of claims that might happen and frequently do. This meant that in order to mitigate or reduce the value of the claim, or to keep a lid on the payment of indemnity dollars, I needed to establish negligence on the part of the injured party to the highest degree possible. Under the Structural Work Act that was not possible.

By virtue of the additional insurance endorsement and contractual language in the contract between the general contractor and the subcontractor--the employer of the injured party--the insurance company was obliged to defend the general contractor for any claims forthcoming from this job that were related to the subcontractor's activity on the job. The more negligence that could be assigned to the claimant, the better. In theory, the sub-contractor agrees to defend the general contractor, not for the general contractor's negligence, but for their own negligence, which can encompass lack of supervision, improper training, a lack of attention for safety concerns, and deviation from industry norms as they relate to safety and proper working procedures.

A general contractor typically holds his/her own liability policy. This is significant because even though a subcontractor, through their carrier, agrees to defend a general contractor or other entity in control of the job site, the general contractor could not, by contract, shift his responsibility or culpability or negligence to another party. Subsequently, the general contractor's carrier was also obliged to defend the general contractor for their own negligence.

In this particular case, the general contractors president admitted that they had held no safety meetings on the job. He also affirmed and acknowledged that they had only hired the best contractors (meaning the carpentry subcontractor), and they had relied on the subcontractors to disseminate ideas and information about safety to their own men. This was an admission that would cost the general contractors carrier significantly in the final analysis. In essence, we had three crosscurrents clashing in this case. One was the issue of the claimant's negligence, the second was the subcontractor's negligence, and the third was the oversight of the general contractor for relying on their carpentry subcontractor to handle safety issues alone.

In this case the defense and indemnification offered by the subcontractor's carrier is limited in scope. It was against public policy to shift by contract one party's negligence to another. Currently a method to circumvent this obstacle is to frame the language in the additional insured endorsement in such a way as to state that the subcontractor's coverage will be the only insurance to address claims forthcoming from a particular construction job, regardless of who has been negligent or to what degree. The law has changed in Illinois whereas a general contractor targets a specific sub-contractor to defend and indemnify the general contractor, even for the general contractor's negligence. These types of cases never get settled quickly. It often takes years of litigation to resolve these sorts of cases, particularly when they involve severe injuries. Initially, the workers' compensation carrier, in a serious case, is called upon to pay the maximum amount of money mandated by law in the state of Illinois, and the comp carrier will likely try like hell—assiduously—to recover some of their lien.

The comp carrier has a 1-B provision providing liability coverage for an employer, if in fact the employer is brought into the lawsuit. 1-A coverage covers injury to an employee, 1-B provides a different type of coverage within the same insurance policy. This is common—coverages in any policy are broken up into sections. When one defendant sues an employer for contribution, this means they are essentially asking the employer to pay part of the settlement to the claimant. The employer, under a commercial general liability policy, usually has another layer of protection beyond the liability coverage afforded by the comp carrier. Things become very complicated with all the various parties pointing their fingers at everyone else. When there is an accident on a large construction site, there are often multiple defendants. The largest I saw involved 16 different, but legitimate, defendants.

Montgomery Board

My clients over the years have almost always been pleased with my results, including an insurance company for whom I would save $75,000. A fellow working at Montgomery Ward, in Lombard, Illinois, had broken his shoulder when he'd fallen from a platform which was lacking proper barricades. Inventory had been stored on this platform, which was in the warehouse area of the store where the public was not allowed. The platform had partially collapsed when this man, who had been hired to stock shelves, was trying to retrieve a particular item.

Alleged to have been built by an independent contractor who had been hired by the store to do general renovations, the plat-form had been in use for at least six months when the accident happened. The contractor identified an employee at the store that worked behind the scenes as a maintenance person and handy-man, putting together displays and shelving. A suit was filed, but the contractor was not able to gain access to the store so they could examine the damaged area. Meanwhile, the employee had collected workers' compensation, and a lien was assigned for more than $20,000. The injured fellow was only in his early 20s, but his shoulder had not healed well.

After I quizzed the contractor about the scope of the their role, it became clear that the renovations had not included the platform the claimant had fallen from. I was convinced the contractor was not responsible for the injury, but not 100 percent so, as I knew they had constructed inventory shelving as part of the job.

I made an appointment to talk to the store's risk manager. My gut feeling was that they would not cooperate, or even allow us to look around. I was made to wait nearly two hours to see him. While I bided my time, I walked out to the dock area and asked for the employee by name—he was the "handyman" Someone pointed out his office to me, and while I did not find him there, someone went to let him know I was waiting in his office. Rather than send me to the corporate office, he sat down and behaved in a congenial manner. Over the course of the next hour, he gave me a detailed statement in which he admitted to constructing the platform himself! He knew the injured employee well. I explained that I was from the contractor's insurance company, and he knew them as well—in fact, he had worked with them quite extensively during the renovations.

As he related the details, I learned that the platform had been constructed with wood purchased at a local lumber yard. He admitted that he had built the platform by himself, without any help from the contractor. I tried very hard not to show my surprise when he told me that the store manager had given him permission to complete the project himself. Because he knew about the injury, and the fact that the contractor had nothing to do with the platform, he was surprised when I told him that the case was in litigation. He smiled, said he was glad to help, and he signed the statement. Naturally, his superiors were furious with him once they got word that he had spilled the beans. A few months later, the carrier asked me to do a follow-up with the man again to make sure he was still around. By that time, his demeanor had shifted to cool and unfriendly.

I was pleased to hear that the plaintiff's attorney had described me as a "damn good investigator." The case was withdrawn and the lawsuit dropped after the "handyman" was deposed. Both the store and their attorney knew that the contractor, the target of the lawsuit, had not been the culprit. Nevertheless, they'd allowed the charade to continue as long as they could.

Buried Alive

In the north suburbs of Chicago, an excavator was working on a three-acre site preparing six home foundations. Each home was to be on a half acre, and each would open at $800,000. The excavation outfit was run by two brothers, who were both very seasoned workers, and usually had a couple of laborers working with them. Unfortunately, the brothers made a mistake that resulted in the loss of life of one of them. My contact at Rockland Casualty insurance company advised me to investigate the situation care-fully as the general contractor was also serving as the property's developer--the general contractor/developer owned the property.

When excavations are made more than six feet below grade, the Occupational Safety Health Agency (OSHA) mandates that shoring material be put up to prevent a collapse of dirt. As they were digging one day, one of the brothers was in a trench when a huge mound of dirt cascaded inside. The trench collapsed, asphyxiating the man. The rest of the crew tried valiantly to save him, but by the time they got him uncovered, he was long gone.

Before I contacted OSHA and found out what their report stated about the incident, I made arrangements to meet the surviving brother. It was two weeks after the accident and he was avoiding me, so I went out to the job without an appointment and urged him to sit down with me. I also talked to one of his employees. The man had been through a tragedy, and I certainly wanted to avoid coming across as cold-hearted. But my job was to establish that he had made a major mistake in judgment, therefore causing his own brother's death. I skirted the issue of the barricades and supports or shoring material, but I found out that he was not aware of the OSHA regulations. He had never even considered putting up shoring material, which somewhat alleviated the general contractor's' culpability. After all, subcontractors are hired for their expertise in a particular field, and it is assumed that the contractor should know how to do his job safely and efficiently.

This was clearly a Structural Work Act case, and the general contractor's carrier was going to have to pay out a pretty good-sized settlement to the deceased's 29-year-old widow and his three children under the age of 6. In addition, the employers insurance carrier would probably have to pay out a sizable sum of money based on the negligence of the surviving brother.

Folks in the construction field must have thick skin, particularly principals or owners, because contractors are almost constantly being sued or suing someone else. This ubiquitous flurry of litigation goes beyond accident cases. On the other hand, at least they are somewhat insulated because very few companies in the construction trades are self-insured. The carriers take a lot of the sting out of the litigation process.

I Hear You Knocking

In the late 80s, there were a few law firms in operation handling plaintiff cases exclusively who seemed to lack any vestige of scruples. They were quite blatant and not very circumspect; in fact, they were almost declaring their position loud and clear: "We dare you to stop us!"

If I were a plaintiff's attorney, I would never, under any circumstances, allow an insurance adjuster to take a statement from a client. I would not, for that matter, even allow an interview. This decision would not preclude a relatively fast settlement, and one is simply giving too much away for free or leaving too much to chance by allowing such a move. Nevertheless, some notorious firms routinely produced clients for statements during this period, which gave an experienced adjuster like me a chance to poke craters in their cases. First of all, a shrewd judge of character could quickly ascertain whether a claimant would make a good or bad witness. Second, by asking questions not anticipated by an attorney, someone like me can catch both client and attorney in a vulnerable position where information not intended for public consumption would leak out. Let's just say that from the plaintiff's point of view, a lot of bad things can happen when you consent to an interview or statement.

One such case concerned a fellow who lived in a predominantly Hispanic neighborhood, though he was not Hispanic. At 38-years-old, he lived with his mother. Lured by one of those famously obnoxious late-night TV advertisers, he hired a firm to do some home repair and remodeling, and replace porches. In turn, the parent company hired small-time contractors to do the actual work, though they had no liability insurance, which is, frankly, incredible, though it's an all too common scenario. In this case, the contractor had insurance with a company that hired me. I called the plaintiff's attorney and told him we would not consider the merits of his case without the opportunity to inter-view and take a statement from his client. He agreed, and the interview took place in his private office, which looked like some antechamber in the Palais d'Versailles, complete with a table worthy of the one Clemenceau had signed the armistice agreement on after World War 1. There was also a painting of three nude nymphs in a forest, with very muted colors except for their backsides. Sir Lancelot would surely have assisted these damsels in distress.

The injured party, Frankie Favela, came across poorly in my view. I immediately sensed he was not only holding back information, but that Mr. Favela had been coached by his attorney before I had been summoned to his magnificent office. After the interview, the attorney told me, "Go back to your principal and instruct them that this case is worth at least a hundred thousand dollars." He assured me that he would have all the medical bills and reports available quickly, and he was eager to begin the negotiation process. I bluntly told him that I felt he had coached his client quite well, and that I wasn't done with my investigation. Without coming out and saying he was full of horse manure, I think he knew I was being sarcastic. I just wanted him to know I wasn't buying into his story just yet.

As the facts came out, it became clear that when they had rebuilt the porch, they had done a fine job with the carpentry work, but the wrought-iron railings had not been secured properly. At least that was the allegation. Mr. Favela related the story that he had been taking a smoke break and had been leaning against the north railing on the porch when it broke. He had fall-en straight down onto the neighbor's catwalk, which was a concrete sidewalk.

No one had witnessed the incident, according to the claimant. A neighbor had found him, but he did not know her name. Naturally, Favela said he'd had no idea the railing was not secured properly, and the fall had taken place 11 and a half months after the work had been completed. Before the interview, I had spoken to our insured and I'd been told that the railing had been checked after the job had been completed—it was very secure. By this time, I have to admit the attorney had raised my competitive hackles with his show of ego and arrogance. The client was too obtuse to be anything but a pawn in his game, despite his severe injuries, a skull fracture, which bothered me as well. The residual problems he was facing after the fall were not surprising. One year later he was still somewhat disoriented, and he was experiencing severe migraine headaches.

Still bent on finishing my job, I went out to the site one night and tracked down the neighbor who had found Frankie Favela on her walkway. She never told me why exactly, but it was obvious that she didn't care too much for her injured neighbor. Regardless, it was apparent she was speaking the truth. According to her account of the events that night in April, there had been a loud, constant pounding noise around 7:30 p.m. After two or three minutes, she finally looked out her window and saw Favela slamming the top side of the railing on the north side of the porch with a large headed hammer. She went back inside her apartment and contemplated calling the police because she was afraid to confront Favela herself. The noise was deafening, she said. Moments later, the noise finally stopped, and the woman looked out again to see Favela sprawled out on her catwalk, blood oozing from his head. I couldn't find anyone else to talk to in the neighborhood, though I was sure there were others who had heard the pounding. Maybe they'd even taken a peek, but only this lady had come forward.

In the end, the carrier offered a small nuisance value settlement which was rejected. The case ended up in court. The witness statement was used to impeach the testimony of the claimant, and Favela received nothing. Not a dime. The mystery of Favela's pounding was never solved, and he never admitted to having done so, but the inspection of the porch revealed the impression of a blunt, hard instrument that had clearly made con-tact with the railing on the top and sides of the railing, lending credence to the witness's story.

Look Ma, No Hands!

Injured-wrist cases are very common. I was told about the case of a woman who had broken both wrists and had worn casts for eight weeks. It was so bad, her husband had to dab her nether regions after each of her bowel movements. When it came time to settle, my associate at the time had given them a little more because he'd felt sorry for them.. They were quite reasonable, really, when it came to making the settlement. The woman had fallen in a grocery store—pop had spilled in one of the aisles because the cans were not stacked properly.

Another woman working for a luggage store in Wilmette, Illinois, severed a tendon in her wrist when she accidentally bumped into a mirror and it collapsed on her. The allegation was that the mirror had been installed improperly by our insured, a glass and mirror installer. The storeowner, even though he had several employees, had no workers' compensation insurance coverage, so the injured employee wanted us, the insurance company, to pay her claim. The facts of the incident were questionable at best, and the woman was exasperated because of our refusal to voluntarily pay her claim, so she hired an attorney. The employer ended up paying more than $100,000 out of his own pocket. The argument was that the employer had moved the mirror himself, after it was installed, thus making it his own fault.

Finishing Touch

Not all work-related cases involve injuries to living beings. Property damage and the like can result in hysteria worthy of grand opera. But buildings and objects need cleaning and maintenance. Machinery needs chemicals to operate, some of which are toxic. Many of the cases I've worked on have had potentially very dangerous repercussions.

The "work product exclusion" relates to insurance coverage regarding a commercial general liability policy. It applies primarily to contractors, but there are small businesses, such as a janitorial service, where "work product" can be a key factor. A good example was when a masonry contractor built a wall on a new construction project for a warehouse. Before they could brace the wall properly, a strong wind blew the wall down, damaging a different contractor's equipment. Two workers were also injured trying to get out of the way as the wall collapsed. They were working for a contractor doing electrical wiring, and had nothing to do with the construction of the wall.

The wall, of course, was reconstructed at the expense of the contractor who built it, and the resultant damage to the equipment, and the injuries of the two workers, were covered by the commercial general liability policy up to the limits set forth in the policy.

In a similar situation, a company was providing janitorial services to a commercial office building. As the janitorial workers were cleaning a terrazzo floor in the lobby of a building, they realized that the chemicals they had used discolored the floor. Nothing could be done to restore the finish. The floor, by definition, was their work product. However, in their policy, they had an endorsement to provide limited coverage for such an eventuality. The floor was replaced, and some depreciation was applied. There was a deductible applied, and the loss was covered up to about 80 percent. This solution satisfied both the building management and the insured. Rather than risk losing a good client, the insured paid the difference and made the client whole. The insured paid an extra premium for this coverage; without it, they might have had to pay 100 percent out of their own coffers, or whatever they could negotiate.

I have not seen many instances where contractors have that work product exclusion override written into the policy. Maybe it is worth the extra expenditure. The only downside is the dollar amount on the coverage is limited, so it won't help if there is big loss.

Insurance costs loom large for small businesses. My experience tells me that many agents don't understand the work product exclusion, even though they may have that override coverage available to sell. Some companies offer it and others don't. I know that many contractors don't understand the concept, either. When I tell them they may not have coverage, they look at me like I've sprouted a second head! The often- heard response is: "Why buy insurance and pay so much for it, and now find out there is no coverage to fall back on?"

Leaks and Bounds

I was asked to handle three chlorine-leak cases in my career. One had occurred at an outdoor swimming pool. When gas had come spewing out in a semi-enclosed area near the pool, 60 people had taken off running up an adjacent hill. It was described to me as something like a "scene in a Charlie Chaplin movie." Chlorine gas is extremely dangerous after just a few seconds of exposure, but everyone had been taken to the hospital and given a clean bill of health. The second case involved a printing company who used chlorine; their backup system had malfunctioned and the entire building in downtown Chicago had been evacuated. No one had been hospitalized, save a couple of the insured employees. Their idea had been to tap into workers' compensation coverage. There were also some sizable business interruption claims----all were denied. Spontaneous leakage of gas is not covered under the policy because of the pollution exclusion, so the carrier refused all of the claims.

In the case regarding the swimming pool, I had been instructed not to stand on the pollution exclusion. After an investigation, we determined that the chlorine-gas supplier had given the health club a tank with a faulty valve. In the end, I settled the case and the gas supplier reimbursed the insurance carrier for every cent paid out.

The third chlorine-gas incident took place in a northern Chicago suburb, where a butcher had a small store in the downtown district. His walk-in freezer, old and antiquated, ran on chlorine gas. The leak was sizable; if someone had lit a match nearby, an explosion could have taken out a city block. More than 25 municipalities responded with fire equipment and personnel, and it took the entire day and night to restore normalcy. Several neighboring businesses would have substantial interruption losses.

A service contractor had given the unit the okay less than a month before the leak. Citing the pollution exclusion, the insurance company providing liability coverage for the business declined coverage. The bill for the fire department response was more than $200,000 alone. The question of business interruption was a separate issue entirely. All coverage was denied, and the butcher was forced to declare bankruptcy. I felt some empathy for the man. He had been a fixture in the downtown area for 40 years when his whole world collapsed.

Oral Wreck

A man working at a state-of- the-art printing and distribution center for a large Chicago newspaper experienced a very bad accident. I was hired to represent the carrier for a subcontractor. The root of the problem was that a subcontractor had left the cover off of a drain pipe, which was only nine inches in diameter. The man working for the newspaper had been operating a rolling scaffold. The wheels of the scaffold had hit the drain opening, and because there was no cover, it had tipped over, causing the employee to fall 15 feet onto a concrete floor and break his jaw. He had also suffered a fractured left clavicle, along with some other nagging injuries that did not require surgery. Workers' compensation benefits had been provided, and had essentially been used to finance his third-party claim against the general contractor and other contractors.

Incredibly, the man and his wife made the odd decision to publicize their sexual proclivities in their deposition. One of the counts in the lawsuit was for loss of consortium. In other words, the husband could not fulfill his sexual duties. The wife explained, in graphic detail, what they were no longer able to do in the privacy of their bedroom as a result of the accident, after his jaw had been wired. Apparently, the missus had a particular affinity for oral sex, and was not in the least bit squeamish about sounding the clarion call about it. Word had it her hubby enjoyed the activity as well. Both husband and wife went into graphic detail about how they partook in this activity several times a week prior to the accident. Now, they felt cheated. Almost as an afterthought, the man mentioned how very awkward it was to eat with his jaw wired shut, too.

I couldn't tell whether their attorney approved of such tactics. If he did, he should have found another line of work. The gambit failed miserably. The sympathy factor prevalent in many cases was not there at all for the jury. Under ordinary circumstances, the couple could have been compensated very well; but after the lurid, prurient and lewd account of what they did behind closed doors, the jury had been offended rather than sympathetic. The end result of their flawed strategy was a settlement that could have been exponentially more had they kept their collective mouths shut, both literally and figuratively. As a plaintiff, you must assiduously refrain from pissing off a jury.

Apparently, work-related injuries can have far-reaching implications. To each his own, I say, though I must admit that case surprised me more than any other.

CHAPTER 8: BLAME IT ON THE WEATHER

Weather plays a large part in how many claims are generated. During the cold months, the more snow and ice there is, the more slip and fall cases seem to follow. In the heat of the summer, some people seem to lose their sense of reason in an effort to stay cool. I have investigated countless claims where nature was a prominent factor. Most have been settled, but rarely where there is an admission of full liability.

In the winter of 2000, we had a nasty storm on February 18th. Two days after the storm, melting occurred, and then nighttime freezing set in. A fellow, who is a truck driver living in an apartment complex in the northwest suburb, was on his way to work at 5:30 a.m. Snow and ice had collected on the walkway to the parking lot, creating a hazard. It was still dark, and the vapor lighting giving off an orange glow did an adequate job of illuminating the sidewalk, but the guy said that he'd never seen the ice. He went down hard and broke his ankle, which required surgery—an "open reduction" procedure. The doctors had to insert hardware into his ankle to ensure reasonable healing.

The maintenance people at the 30-year-old apartment complex were aware of this problem, and a plan was just about to be implemented regarding the cracks, holes and concrete settlement problems in the walkways. The fellow who fell was a relatively new tenant and had not seen such conditions before. The complex was fairly well maintained, and there were no complaints to management by any of the 12 tenants who lived there relative to problems with ice-buildup in the area in question. The problem was, the concrete had settled and had sunken six inches.

First and foremost, we did not want this fellow to gravitate to an attorney. He was a rather simple man, but his wife was much more inquisitive than he. He never did hire an attorney. He was off of work for three and a half months, and he had disability insurance through his work that paid 50 percent of his salary. After two surgeries within seven days of the accident, he actually made a decent recovery despite a nasty smoking habit. He even remarked that the doctor had told him that smoking would retard the healing process.

I settled his case for $17,500---he was happy. We never received a lien from his employer, their hospitalization carrier, or their disability carrier, but I told him that he might have to pay them back out of the settlement. This case, with shrewd attorney representation, was worth at least $75,000, if not more. Later on, I was saddened to learn that his wife had left him. He was simple, but he wasn't stupid. I guess accumulating money was not a major part of his agenda.

The Dangers of a Spring Breeze

In 1995, we had a stretch of weather in Chicago that had the global warming pundits saying, "I told you so!" In early March, we had ten days straight hovering in the 60s and low 70s. After that nice little run, the weather went back to normal, which was in the low 40s for the daytime high. This lasted until early April. There were a few days that teased us, but after the early March boom, we all suffered, waiting and longing for real spring weather. The fact that nice weather descended on us when it was still officially winter should have reminded us that nothing really nice lasts forever.

Up in Rogers Park, a changing area on the north perimeter of the city near the lake, there are many apartment buildings. There are also some single-family homes and a strong commercial base on Sheridan Road, Howard Street and Clark Street. Many of the apartment buildings are multi-unit dwellings, as opposed to two-or three-unit buildings.

There is also a great Midwestern university set in Rogers Park, named Loyola. Of course, located in Evanston, just north of Rogers Park, Northwestern University rests on the western shores of Lake Michigan. Rogers Park is a very diverse area with an eclectic flavor. The people that live in the single-family homes provide a stable family influence in the area. There is a very solid Jewish population, and many younger folks just starting out after finishing school. Rogers Park has some unstable influences as well, which gained my attention more than one time in my career.

The weather was warm, and I suspect that many of the buildings, not expecting the warm early March weather, were still running the central heating. The building I was asked to investigate had window stoppers—a hardware device installed above the lower window. The lower window would slide open if it was pushed in an upward motion, and the device would only allow the window to open about 12 inches. There were locks on both sides of the windows, but they could be manually disengaged to open the window all the way. If the window were open all the way, there would be a gap of about two and a half to three feet between the windowsill and the bottom of the raised window. This feature gave the tenants flexibility in terms of how much fresh air they wanted.

A female tenant in her early 20s, living alone, was feeling the heat one day. The building hadn't turned off the heat, and the ten-ants had no individual thermostats, which is common in older apartment buildings. Consequently, the tenant had opened a couple of windows in order to create a cross-current from north to south. She was on the first floor and had no east or west facing windows. In her apartment, she had a bank of windows on the south wall that one could see in if she had no blinds or shading covering the windows.

This tenant fell asleep on her sofa on a Sunday afternoon, around 4:00 p.m. Meanwhile, a young black man positioned himself on the south side of her street. It was an east-west street, and he was approximately 40 feet away from her windows. He could see her motionless on the sofa. The man, who turned out to be a rapist, used crude ingenuity to enter through her north window—it was wide open and there was no screen. He went around the north side of the building and found her row of windows, then he pulled or pushed a dumpster over to the area below her window, which was nine feet up. He climbed up on the dumpster and simply crawled through the window while the woman was still asleep. She woke to find him threatening her with a knife. He raped her and left within ten minutes. No one heard a thing.

The criminal was never caught, but was described in detail by the poor woman when she gave a report to the police. A neighbor was comforting her, and what she described had every appearance of a legitimate account of rape. The victim was sobbing, and kept repeating that she couldn't believe what had happened. The neighbor said that the woman was acting as if she was experiencing a bad dream, but still, she was very distraught. The neighbor did not see any signs of a struggle, such as scratches on her arms, legs, or face, and her clothes were not ripped. After the police arrived, the victim was taken to a nearby hospital. My communications with the police suggested that the man might be a serial rapist. Oddly enough, there had been no robbery attempt.

Suit was filed against the building, and the owner informed me that the window locks had been installed a couple of years before this incident. The dumpster stood four feet off the ground, and was for garbage collection for the tenants. It had been in an enclosed courtyard area north of the building. Was the building owner negligent for having the dumpster in an area where a person could use it as a climbing device?

The key ingredient in this case was the fact that the window locks were present and functional. The claimant had overridden the use and function of the locks, never contemplating the potential danger. Was the insured negligent for keeping the heat on during this unprecedented run of fine weather? The heat certainly had to be on at night. Though it was an extremely unfortunate incident, liability imputed to the owner of the building was tenuous at best. The case settled for $18,000 after a couple of pretrial hearings. The carrier's thinking was, if they could buy out reasonably, they would do so, rather than face the specter of what a jury might perceive as the owner's negligence, therefore rendering a potentially much larger judgment to the plaintiff.

Taking the Plunge

In July of 1999, the Chicago area was enveloped in a blistering heat wave. From July 10th through July 29th, the temperature was over 95 degrees every day, and on three or four of those days, it was over 1.00 degrees. There was no let up at all.

One night at around 9:15, my son and I were coming home from playing golf, after eating a quick dinner. We were overjoyed that the temperature was down to 81 degrees. It was a stark change to the oven we had become accustomed to—typically, at 9:00 p.m., it had been between 87 and 90 degrees during the heat wave. The low temperature during any 24-hour period had been between 73 and 75 degrees. It conjured up memories of the summer of 1995, when there had been a similar heat wave, which had resulted in the destruction of many finely-manicured golf courses. Golf superintendents were tearing their hair out over a blight called "pythia"

The PGA Championship was held at Medinah, in the west suburbs, in 1999. About ten days before the official opening of the championship, they made the mistake of cutting the greens too close. The greens were already extremely stressed because of the heat, and the fact that there was no dissolution of that hot weather. Our greens keeper explained to me that there was no cooling off effect at night, which would have occurred if the temperatures had crept down to the middle, or even high 60-degree range.

the porches in question have rotting or have loose boards. To maintain the wood, the porches require diligent maintenance.

Earlier, I recounted the story of a fellow who had tossed a pail of water over a railing, and the momentum had carried his body right through the railing. Because the wood was rotted where it was connected to the brick masonry wall, he had fallen three stories and had suffered multiple fractures. He was lucky considering the fact that he'd landed on concrete, 30 feet below. I have always been extremely leery of these porches, especially above the first floor. I've climbed some that didn't especially inspire confidence in their structural soundness.

In most cases involving porches, the people that fall either go through, over, or in some cases, under railings. That should never happen. In one case I worked on, the entire third-floor porch had come down, causing the second-floor porch to collapse as well. All of the 20 people on the third-floor porch had ended up at ground level, or close to it. The incident happened when three fellows, all roommates, threw a rousing party where they served beer and barbecue. The party occurred on a balmy night in late spring of 1995. Spirits were high and folks were excited by visions of the beautiful weather that would soon be coming to the Midwest in the late spring and summer. There were about 100 people at the party; fortunately, only about 20 people were outside.

My job was to investigate for the carrier. One young lady had broken her neck, though she wasn't paralyzed. Her neck was fit into a halo device for several months, and she made a fairly nice recovery. She did have some more permanent problems in her cervical spine, and she had some emotional scars as well. Another girl had cracked some vertebrae in her back, and she had a ruptured spleen, a fractured wrist, and a broken right femur. Thankfully, she also made a nice recovery, but had some residual problems as people do when they suffer multiple injuries. It was anticipated that she would eventually develop arthritis in her leg and wrist as a result of her fall, and she had hardware surgically inserted in her leg and wrist. The first woman had more than $150,000 in bills; the second woman had over $100,000 in bills. Several other people also had serious injuries that required medical attention over several months. One fellow who had fallen and sustained at least two fractures had about $60,000 in medical bills.

The porch was canted about 10 degrees downward from the back door, leading to the southern edge of the porch toward the stairway, which led to

The condition of the greens at Medinah was a source of great controversy. The bare spots were actually sprayed with a green dye when the tournament began! In spite of the problem, the greens, I'm told, putted fairly true—much better than the greens at the Riviera in 1995, as a matter of fact. Some people called the summer of 1999 the summer from hell, or concrete proof of the global warming effect. I'm sure that people fortunate enough to have swimming pools made good use of them in 1999 during the last two thirds of July.

Around the 10th of August, I received a call from a trusted account regarding a guest at a party who had been seriously injured trying to jump into one of those swimming pools. A young woman of 22 had hosted the get-together with several friends at her parents' house—they were out of town at the time. They were aware that she was using the house, but they weren't thrilled to learn that she had asked 25 people over for a party.

Immediately, the carrier wanted to handle the case under a reservation of rights, and they wanted me to have a non-waiver signed; a non-waiver agreement is signed by the insured, and acknowledges that the carrier has the right under the policy to investigate, and then determine at a later date if coverage would be afforded. If the carrier doesn't do this, then they may be stopped, or prevented, from raising coverage issues in the future regarding a particular accident. The reservation of rights letter outlines specifically what coverage issues are germane to the case, and specifically states actual policy language. Other than attorneys who specialize in interpreting coverage issues, and insurance adjusters who know policies intimately, nobody really understands or cares to understand these issues, truth be told. The letter to the insured is typically sent after the non-waiver agreement is signed.

I told my contact at the company that there was no way they could deny coverage in this instance, because the daughter had been there with the parents' permission. The people at the party were not trespassers. I told the homeowners that I did not believe that their coverage was in jeopardy involving this matter, although I could not tell them unequivocally that it would turn out that way.

I ended up interviewing some 1.2 people regarding this accident. It took me a month to track everyone down. I never got a chance to interview the injured party, though. She was from Ireland, and was not exactly an exchange student, but was here regarding her studies. She had also worked at a north suburban restaurant while in Chicago. I tried to meet with her at

Northwestern Memorial Hospital, but her father, who had come from Ireland to assist her, would not allow me to interview her, even though at that time they had not hired an attorney. Eventually, an attorney took the case and we verbally sparred about the matter. In Illinois, "assumption of risk" is a wildly used defense doctrine, and in this case it was likely to be successful in achieving a summary judgment, directed verdict or a not guilty verdict. There were a few caveats, however.

The party had begun at around 6:30 p.m. on one of those hot, sultry nights ideal for a pool party and barbecue. The host and a couple of her friends had pulled a stunt that still sends shivers up my spine. Apparently, they were taking running leaps off of a roof above the second floor to the water below. Access was gained by crawling out a third floor window onto a slanted roof with a 15-degree pitch. The back of the house measured ten feet to the edge of the water, so by taking a running jump, a person could successfully land in the pool. The drop was 25 feet, and this maneuver was repeated several times by about four people.

The party host had befriended the Irish visitor when they worked together at a health-food restaurant on the north shore. The Irish gal had been working that night, and had arrived at the party around 11:00 p.m. There was liquor at the party, but most, if not all of the guests were 21 or older. The Irishwoman had not been drinking. As soon as she got to the party, though, she was collared by one of the jumpers and urged to give it a try. They went so far as to find a bathing suit for her. She was described by other guests as being not particularly athletic, and a bit over-weight. The host never talked to her before she jumped.

One key item in the investigation that came out during my interviews with several guests was that only a few of them had jumped. The ones that didn't jump said that they felt it had been too dangerous. A couple of people I interviewed said they had thought carefully about it, and had decided that it was far too perilous. "Assumption of risk" means that one goes ahead with a dangerous act, even though they know full well they might experience imminent physical harm. The fellow that urged the Irish girl to jump was pretty lit up with booze. I never got a chance to talk to him. She tried to get a running start, but her momentum wasn't sufficient to clear the deck; she almost made it, but she caught her left leg on the pool's edge. Everyone was in a state of shock when they soon realized that she was seriously injured. After retrieving her from the water, the paramedics were called immediately.

Her left ankle was smashed, and she had fractured several vertebrae in l
lower back.

The host's parents had no idea that their daughter had been doing
jump routine for about five years, but she admitted to it in her testimony
saw it as a "monkey see, monkey do" situation, yet we were talking abou
person well past the age of majority, capable of making informed decisic
for herself.

The medical bills were high—close to $200,000. Thankfully, t
Irishwoman was not paralyzed, though, and after a long rehab, she wou
walk again, but never as gingerly as she had before the accider
Unfortunately, she'd made the choice herself. I gave her attorney a verb
barrage concerning the assumption of risk defense, and I told him the de
was stacked against him. I asked him if he could stand up in front of a jur
with a straight face, and try to convince them that whatever perceiv
negligence there was in the case against the insured from the plaintiff's poi
of view could override the act of stupidity on his client's part. He could pla
on the sympathy aspect—she was in a strange country, cajoled by people sl
hardly knew, to take this flight of fancy. I knew the attorney woul
characterize her as an innocent victim and harp on the severe and permaner
injuries. The attorney admitted off the record that it was worth a sho
because "you never know what a jury will do in Cook County." I knew this t
be true—he had a point. Knowing all of these factors did not make me an
less the aggressor when it came to trying to sow a seed of doubt and dissuad
him from pursuing the matter further, though. The case is still pending.

High Spirits on a Balmy Night

Numerous brick apartment buildings in Chicago and its suburbs were built ir
the 1920s and 1930s. It was a triumph of form and function, because these
buildings, if maintained properly, certainly were long lasting and sturdy.
Most of these two or three-flat buildings have wooden porches, however, that
don't last as long as the buildings do.

I suppose if you paint assiduously, or use Wolmanized wood—a lumber
treated to last longer--a porch can last for 30 to 40 years, but that would be
stretching it. These brick masonry buildings have provided more than
adequate living space for millions of people over the years, and those porches
have also seen their fair share of mishaps over the years. In many instances,

the second floor. It measured 20 feet deep from the backdoor to the stairway, and it was 30 feet wide. It was, of course, constructed of wood, and the owner said that it had not been replaced in at least 20 years.

I was baffled by the fact that I wasn't asked to begin my investigation until 1996, even though the collapse had happened in 1995. Obviously, someone had either sat on this at the carrier, or it had been reported late. Upper management should have started the heads rolling for this heinous oversight. I spoke with several of the people who had been on the porch when it col-lapsed, or who had been on the porch earlier that evening. None of them had felt anything that would suggest the porch was shaky or somehow compromised. I learned, though, that in addition to the 20 people on the porch, there was a large grill and two kegs of beer, weighing well over 300 pounds. There were also people dancing just prior to the collapse. One of the attendees at the party reported hearing a "snapping" noise, and said that the porch started to come down in slow motion, with the section of the porch farthest away from the back door collapsing first.

In 1995, Illinois Tort Reform was passed, limiting noneconomic damages in an injury case to $500,000. That meant that after medical bills were paid and lost income was reimbursed, someone could only get $500,000 to compensate for pain and suffering, aggravation, and diminished lifestyle, which included the inability to physically do something that could be done before the accident.

As of July, 1996, the general perception among attorneys and people in the insurance industry was that the noneconomic damage feature in the Tort Reform Act would be declared unconstitutional and therefore overturned. There was much vehement opposition to the feature from the plaintiff bar. I figured—conservatively—that this young lady, wearing the halo device, would get a settlement of at least $650,000, and maybe upwards of a $1,000,000. The two other serious cases had a conservative value in the $500-$600,000 range, if not more. The fellow with fractures who had $60,000 in medical bills had been unable to work for a year. His lost income was in the $48,000 range. He had suffered a broken leg, a fractured humerus, and a hairline fracture of his right hip. His case was worth over $500,000, and he had, happily, made a fairly nice recovery himself.

The clients in the three most serious injury cases all had sharp attorneys who knew their way around a court of law. As a matter of fact, they routinely tried cases and garnered large settlements. Some cases would not have to be tried, usually because of liability issues being stacked in favor of the plaintiff. This was coupled with the fact that the clients had serious debilitating injuries with permanent residual problems. In essence, these factors made the cases a bonanza for the attorney handling it. I was impressed myself when I interviewed the young lady with the broken neck and halo device, which had been removed. She made a great witness for herself, and I knew a jury would love her.

Significantly, I ended up settling eight or nine of the small injury cases in the $1,000-$5,000 range.

The building itself had $2,000,000 in underlying coverage, with an additional $2,000,000 through an umbrella policy. There was no renter's coverage available. I asked the building owner if he had had any inspections or work done on the porches prior to the collapse. In fact, he had hired a contractor in the fall of 1994, and they had replaced some railings on the porch, though they hadn't touched any of the vertical supports. The contracting company was brought into the case after the original lawsuits were filed as a third party defendant. The allegation was that they should have seen the possibility of a problem, and they should have made recommendations to the owner, either verbally or in writing.

It occurred to me that the porch wasn't meant to hold 20 dancing people with two kegs of beer and a grill. If I had been a party guest, I would have been afraid to stand out there with all that weight and vibration. However, I never felt for a moment that even an extremely sharp defense attorney could convince a jury that the victims were guilty of fault. The carrier for the building obviously had a major problem on their hands. I know for a fact that they had to reserve at least $2,500,000 for this case. I was the bearer of bad tidings for that carrier when I made my report and laid the facts out for them. They already had some inkling of what might be involved prior to getting my report, but my report had brought the problem into very clear focus for them.

The jury verdict reporter stated in 1999 that the young woman with the broken neck had received $700,000 before the case ever went to trial. I never heard what figure the other two bad injury claimants received. The building owner had the porch rebuilt with steel members, and the building was eventually sold for $1,750,000. The contractor who worked on the porch was nicked for $600,000, or at least that's what his insurance carrier paid. There were multiple lawsuits, but not one of the cases ever went to trial. Typically, when suit is filed, a defense attorney will settle a case while in litigation, during a pretrial meeting in the judge's chambers. Or, the case will go to trial and a jury will enter a judgment. In this scenario, the various lawsuits may have been consolidated. After discovery, there are pretrial meetings with the judge and the two sides. The judge can be a strong advocate to persuade the two opposing parties to find middle ground, and that's what happened here: the pre-trial meetings proved to be fruitful. The insurance carrier had every incentive to settle; they didn't want to see any of these cases go to a jury, which could be a real crap shoot in Cook County, especially. With an accident and subsequent injuries like this case had, the jury was likely to be very generous.

Winter Woes: A Tale by an Honest Friend

I wrote this story in this unusual manner to illustrate how a person on the inside perceives a major mess as a result of a flood.

My name is John Krueger. I used to work at the Ritz, one of the most coveted dwellings on the Gold Coast. I worked there as assistant engineer. I decided to leave their employ, though, because the building was truly uninhabitable. I could have kept my job, but things were so chaotic after the great flood disaster that I just needed to find another place to work.

*It wasn't a bad place to work. The people were quite demanding, but the pay was above average and there was always plenty to do. People tip real nicely if you help them with a minor problem. There were 30 floors in the building **with 56** units, and a penthouse on the 29th and 30th floors, all had magnificent views of the lake and the skyline. In early January, the finishing touches were being put on the 29th and 30th floors. Those two floors had been purchased by a really nice man and his wife. By the end of January, they were planning to take possession. The general contractor brought me up there to show **me** a couple of the features they had designed and installed so that if the owner ever needed help with anything, I might be of service to them. The unit was spectacular in every facet, with a small swimming pool and a huge sauna, even! The furnishings were eclectic, with some quite modern 21st century pieces, and others that might be described as "anachronisms." They really had a mix of styles which were adroitly meshed* *and added to the charm. The stainless-steel, modern-art look certainly stood out. The kitchen had all the modern European appliances. It was a chef's delight! They had over $250, 000 in the latest appliances for the culinary aficionado.*

Even though they didn't have a private elevator going all the way up, they did have a private elevator from the 28th floor up to the 29th floor, which they could only gain access to with a passkey card, similar to those issued in a hotel. Rumor has it they paid more than $3, 000, 000 for the place. I overheard one of the contractors who was working up there say that they were spending at least another $3,000,000 to furnish and outfit the two floors. Money was obviously no object.

Everything was pretty quiet at the building in early to middle January. It was a fairly mild winter, but we did have some cold days after very early January. A couple of minor events occurred. One of the tenants came home quite intoxicated and ran into three cars in the garage, doing about $60,000 in damage. All were late-model Mercedes. His own car, a lowly Jaguar, cost about $15,000 to repair. One of the residents on the 21st floor had a dishwasher that leaked, causing some damage to the two units below. When the leak occurred, no one was home, so some people got a big surprise.

I worked a lot of nights there. The residents were willing to pay to have someone there until midnight. I would describe the people in the building as being generally nice in demeanor, but there were a few real pistols, and not many Indians, but a lot of chiefs. This became as apparent as a cold slap in the face after the great disaster.

Around 8:00 a.m. on a cold winter morning, a pipe broke in the 30th floor ceiling. One of the workers from the general con-tractor was already in the penthouse. I was not on duty at the time, but was awakened and asked to come. It was a weekday. The chief engineer went up to the unit to ascertain the problem instead of simply shutting the water supply off for the entire building. He admitted to me later that he had panicked. The water ran, for 30 to 35 minutes. The buss bar in the building that supplies the electricity to all the various units was severely saturated. The units all the way down to the fifth floor were damaged. This was a 25-year-old building, of course.

The power was cut off for about a day, and within a couple of days, the full breadth of the damage was becoming apparent. Within a week, systems in the building weren't working so well. **One** *of the elevator banks was shut down because of the excessive moisture. Many units were damaged with* *personal possessions bearing the brunt. Mildew was setting in. People in the building were in an uproar! Many off the building's inhabitants were in Florida, but several had stayed for the winter: The Ritz Carlton **and** The Drake, and other fine hotels in the area, picked up some new and steady patrons. There were not enough suites to satisfy the displaced refugees. After two weeks, the building was basically vacant, with the only inhabitants being a skeleton crew. The place was crawling with insurance adjusters and property damage experts. Some guy was up in the penthouse the day after the flood videotaping the pipe that burst and the damage on the 30th floor.*

I was having a beer with a friend of the ex-building engineer who remarked that he was surprised he d lasted three months after this event occurred. Finally he couldn't take it anymore and he quit. He had received a lot of negative feedback from the board and the unit owners, and he intimated that when the building was finally completely open (three months after it was shut down), the hotel bills totaled over $1.5 million for the displaced residents. The building was finally shut down completely on February 1, 1999.

Having been therefor a month and a half after the building shut down, I had witnessed the chaos and ugliness myself. The buss bar had been destroyed, and there were two estimates to replace it, one of them being for over a million dollars. There was also a rumor that a famous sports star who lived in the building had contributed to damaging the buss bar because of his leaking fish tank, which held a thousand gallons of water. That seems unlikely, though. I had never heard of that sort of complaint before.

Almost everyone in the building owned their units, so they couldn't just walk away, and there was rampant speculation about who exactly was responsible for the pipe bursting. I went there myself to see what it looked like. I'm not an expert, but I have a good basic knowledge of mechanical systems, including heating and cooling, and I could see that the pipe that burst had been a water supply pipe for the sprinkler system. I guessed that it had burst because there was not enough insulation in the 30th floor ceiling. During the few days before the disaster, the temperature had been close to zero degrees Fahrenheit. I also saw a heating register in the ceiling with the connection unfastened. The connection would distribute heat evenly in the ceiling, preventing freezing conditions for the pipes.

I know for a fact that some changes were made in the ceiling below the 30th floor roof for mechanical systems before the accident. There was a *heating and air conditioning contractor working as a sub for the general contractor on the project for the 29th and 30th floors. After the flood, I also noticed missing insulation on the north wall above the ceiling, below the roof, no more than ten feet from the burst pipe. No one had ever come to talk to me about it, so I felt a little bit left out. Once I was gone from the building, I could have given one of those insurance adjusters an earful!*

Something odd happened during the following summer I ran into the current manager of the building at Wrigley Field. The Cubs won that day, 1-0 over Houston in spite of the wind blowing out at 30 miles an hour. The winning run was "balked" in. So, the manager told me that several lawsuits had been filed regarding the flood, and he figured the entire damage from a monetary standpoint, including damage to the units, would exceed $20,000,000. The general contractor's carrier was reluctant to accept blame for something they believed was the fault of two or three subcontractors.

He also commented that the entire matter would not be resolved for at least ten years.

CHAPTER 9: NO ONE EVER SAID IT **WOULD BE EASY**

There are obviously a number of very hazardous careers—police work, firefighting, construction work and driving a cab are considered to be lines of work that carry inherent dangers under a variety of circumstances. Some folks would assume that a fellow like me has it pretty easy. Anyone unfamiliar with the tasks I must perform on a daily basis might think I spend a lot of time behind a desk, or sitting in a car, making notes and biding time. This simply isn't so. In my 30 years on the job, I've found myself in situations ranging from the humorous and bothersome to the downright life-endangering. Scenarios always seem less frightening in retrospect, but I've seen my life flash before my eyes on several occasions. There's no down-playing the dangers of so-called "victims" on a mission, either. In hindsight, I laugh, but I've certainly learned some important life lessons, one being that some folks are just plain nuts.

Head on a Swivel

On October 19, 1995, I got stuck in downtown Chicago in the late afternoon, which meant getting to the western suburbs would be a crawl. I remembered an accident scene that needed to be scoped and photographed on the near west side, so I decided to venture off the expressway and check the intersection out. It was around 4:00 p.m. when I left the expressway going north and west about six blocks. Typically, on such a fine day, I would have been on the golf course at that hour. I could have left the down-town area earlier, but I had wanted to finish something rather than go back the next day.

People were outside en masse that day as it was almost 80 degrees. Initially, I had thought that the most prudent way to handle my duties was to view the intersection in the early morning, or to wait for the temperature to drop precipitously, so a chill in the air would keep the masses inside. This particular area, at Washington and Kilbourn, was known for its gang activity at the time. I drove north on Kilbourn toward Washington, where I saw 30 to 40 young men congregating on the northwest corner, doing nothing in particular. I stopped the car and took two photographs facing north. Then I got back in the car and made it to Washington. I wanted to go east to get out of there; I dared not go north of Washington on Kilbourn, although if there had been no one there, I would have stopped a half a block north of Washington to take photographs of the view facing south on Kilbourn. I was doing this to show the intersection from all four angles and I was planning to stop again after going east on Washington to take a couple of photos facing west, but unfortunately, my plans were interrupted.

Apparently, one of the fellows on the northwest corner must have thought that I was taking pictures of them as a group to finger them with the Chicago Police. He came running at me like a track star with a ten-foot long jagged piece of plywood shaped like a spear or javelin. Traffic was slow going eastbound, so I was going nowhere fast. Finally, he caught up with me. My windows were down, and the guy flung the sharp object through my passenger window, just missing my nose. The front end of the spear ended up outside my driver's window.

In an effort to maneuver away from this maniac, I drove into oncoming traffic and narrowly missed a couple of cars going westbound. Luckily, there were no parked vehicles on the north side of Washington, so I drove on that lane, going eastbound and traveling the wrong way. Eventually, I made it 300 or 400 yards away from this miscreant. I ended up well east of where he was, in the curb lane on the south side of the street. He was standing there glaring at me as I got out of the car. Traffic had cleared. I got out of the car, pulled the spear out and broke it over my knee, and I threw it in his direction in a gesture of defiance. I also gave him a rather uncomplimentary gesture and shouted some obscenities, which I was fairly certain he could hear. Then I got back in my car, went to the next block, and turned south. I went to Madison Street though my inner voice was telling me that I should just leave.

By that time, I had controlled my breathing, conquered my fear, and rage had started to well up inside of me. It was extremely bad judgment to have put myself in that situation in the first place. I had violated my cardinal safety rule: if it doesn't look safe or feel safe, I don't proceed. I have a strong intuition which serves me well, but I ignored my instincts that day and nearly paid for my mistake with my life.

On the day this happened, I was highly irritable, and I frankly cannot remember why. When I feel this way, I confess I become very stubborn. In retrospect, I didn't need to tempt fate as I had because I would have been in the same general area in the next couple of days. I also knew the weather was about to change dramatically to much colder temperatures, a better option when it comes to going into a high-crime area. Nevertheless, I wanted to get this done on the way back to civilization. I charge more money for going into crime-ridden areas simply because I put myself at risk. Frequently, the nightly news reports drive-by shootings of innocent bystanders caught in gang warfare crossfire. My original plan was to spend 30 minutes getting my photos. I have always thought it makes good business sense to maximize time.

Stubbornness is generally productive for me, but it also occasionally gets me in a fix that I should be smart enough to avoid. I decided, as I turned on Madison Street, to go westbound, and not to go back to the expressway immediately. But I was not going to let these gang bangers push me around or dictate where I could go or what I could do. That inner voice built itself into a cacophonous noise in my brain, telling me that if they couldn't take a joke, fuck 'em! So I went back toward the intersection on the west side of Kilbourn, on Washington. I ended up three quarters of a block west of Kilbourn, facing east, and I pulled over near where the parked cars would be on the south side of the street. I got out of the car and looked furtively to see if anyone was around. I saw no one, and there was little or no traffic in either direction. As I got out, I left the door open, and I snapped two photos facing east on Washington, west of Kilbourn. I turned around, and was only out of the car for about 20 seconds. Suddenly, much to my chagrin, there was a guy trying to drive my car away! He was in his 20s, average height, and about 180 pounds. Now he had a problem. He didn't know how to drive a manual transmission. He stalled the car, and was desperately trying to restart it. I knew it wasn't the same guy who had thrown the spear.

In a semi-state of shock, I told him to get the fuck out of my car, and I moved toward him. I screamed that the police were coming, and he engaged me in a wrestling match, just outside the car. Somehow, in the scuffle, he got my camera and cell phone. In the ensuing struggle, I was able to get back in the car while he was still pummeling me. The keys were still in the ignition. He had already kicked me in the upper right thigh, a kick that had been designated for my groin, but he'd missed narrowly. I was sitting in the driver's seat with my legs outside the car when I received the blow. I managed to shut the door and was trying to start the car while he was still pummeling me in the face with his fist. I just kept yelling, "The police are coming!"

I finally got the car started and I drove off, first driving east. He let go of the door. Then, I saw about 10 or 15 of his comrades running west toward me. They were about 150 yards away, so I made a U-turn, cutting off a car going west on Washington. At that point, I was going westbound on Washington, and the fellow I had struggled with threw my cell phone at the car. He missed, and I made a sharp maneuver to get around him without running him down. I ended up in oncoming traffic, so I swerved back sharply to my right, back into my westbound lane, just missing a viaduct support. I barely made my escape. The guy had broken off my cruise control arm, he'd taken my camera, which wasn't all that expensive, and my cell phone was lying in the street.

I went west to Cicero, and made a left to go south so I could put some distance between myself and that neighborhood. In the town of Cicero, just south of the expressway, I found a pay phone and called Cellular One to cancel my account. Needless to say, I was pretty shaken up. I was scratched and a little sore, but I was okay. Hard to believe that I hadn't hit anyone or anything under those circumstances.

I also wondered where the police had been all this time. In Illinois, a law had been introduced with Chicago in mind about dispersing gangs, stating that no more than two people could congregate on a street corner at any given time. Later, the law was declared unconstitutional. I think the American Civil Liberties Union challenged it, claiming that it was a violation of the first amendment and personal and civil rights.

Every story has an ending of sorts. I put closure on this one by going by the intersection two days later, when the temperature had dropped to around 40 degrees. Much to my amazement, there were still 30 of them out on the corner. I was driving a different car, and I went north on Kilbourn and then east on Washington and got the hell out of there. Had the place been deserted, I'm still not sure if I would have mustered the courage to take the photos.

Verbal Diarrhea

I'm a "can-do" guy. If someone needs a difficult task done, I'm the man to give it to. I've always had that reputation, and for all I know, I still do. After a lady (and I use the term loosely) viciously cussed several people out, including two VPs, in the claims department at a major company, they decided to hand the case over to an independent adjuster and let them take the abuse. And abuse we took—a heavy ration of it.

I had five people working for me at the time, and every one of them took a double shot of this woman's particular brand of verbal ferocity. I experienced the bulk of it because it was my main intention to settle her claim and insulate my people. It took me six months to get it done.

This "lady," Maribel Fernandez, had been rear-ended in her automobile, resulting in $2700 in damage to her car alone. She also claimed to have soft tissue injuries to her neck and back, and she complained of strange tingling in her hands, which she attributed to the physical trauma of the accident. After two months of verbal sparring, I finally got her to sign a consent form so I could write to her doctor, but it didn't do much good. The doctor simply could not figure out what was wrong with her and he also was on the verge of refusing to treat her because she swore at him mercilessly. I had to wonder how she treated her superiors at the department store where she worked. I suspected that she was very much in tune with exactly who she could cuss out and who would simply not tolerate her behavior, which reminded me of a recalcitrant teenager who acts up at home, but not in the outside world. Fernandez claimed that she had spent $600 on Advil alone—she was popping at least 15 of them a day. The biggest component of her claim, though, was her assertion that she'd lost a promotion at work because of her inability to perform at peak levels. In other words, the accident had ruined her life.

I didn't give Fernandez a lot of thought, beyond grappling with her weekly tirades. To be frank, it had become quite comical after a while. I finally had the pleasure of meeting her when I delivered the settlement check. If looks could maim, I would have been in big trouble. She clearly hated my guts. I had won, though, because I'd tolerated her nastiness. Basically, through patience, I'd gotten her to cease and desist. An investigator becomes sort of a psychologist, and my theory was that Maribel, who was 30 years old, just needed someone to belittle. She was obviously projecting and demonstrating her own pain and insecurity. It became apparent to me that she had come from an abusive background, but that she'd become a bully instead of a victim. It was clear that her husband, an older fellow who was rather meek and laid-back, didn't wear the pants in the family. She obviously used him as her own personal pin cushion. I wondered if she ever did anything to make him smile. Thank God, and no wonder, they had no children.

After the settlement was completed, one of the people she had terrorized at the company (who had initially handled her claim) talked to me. She told me the settlement I'd made was too generous, though the company was thrilled that they'd seen the last of the abusive lady. Of course, she wasn't aware of all of the variables that had been considered in making the choice to resolve the issue. She only knew the final figure. A year later, I found out that this same critic had been indicted for taking kick-backs from attorneys. Her criticism had never caused me to lose any sleep--I knew I'd solved a major nuisance problem. It was terribly ironic, though, that the insurance company employee who criticized me turned out to be a felon.

I apologized to all of my employees who had been forced to experience Fernandez's foul mouth. They weren't squeamish by any means, but I tried to commiserate with them so that they knew I was always on their side.

Fernandez was impossible to forget because her behavior was so far from the norm. I realized after dealing with her that I would never take crap from anyone without giving them something to chew on. JJ McGillicuddy had been a consummate actor—he should have gone into politics. But he would drown his sorrows in the bottle, especially as he got older. He hated confrontations. He'd been an important role model for me during the beginning of my career, but now I'd decided I needed to fire back sometimes with some of these objectionable people. It was a matter of saving my own sanity. By getting some pent-up hostility off my chest, I never had to go out and beat my dog or, worse yet, take it out on my family. Plus, I avoided the booze brigade.

When Negotiations Get Personal

I was in an attorney's office interviewing a client one day. While I was there, I was approached by a paralegal asking if I would conclude a case that we had been discussing for a month or so, in hopes of resolving it right then and there. The attorney delegated a lot of authority to this paralegal, so I primarily talked to her. The big disagreement was over money, as usual. I offered $18,500, and they wanted $23,000. I couldn't justify more than $20,000, but I wanted to settle for under that figure. Without going into elaborate detail, the case was worth $20,000, so settling it under that amount would secure me a "gold star," a euphemism for receiving more business.

The paralegal was not my type—I wasn't particularly attracted to her—

but I could see where others might be. She was attractive if you like glitz and flash, which does little for me. I've always liked a girl from the Midwest who doesn't need a lot of makeup because she is pretty in a natural way—not many women can actually pull that off. A rather subtle proposal was made. In exchange for more settlement dollars, $4,500 more to be exact, she was ready to provide sexual favors for me of the most lascivious nature. Now, I am not completely immune to these types of advances, but I have a beautiful wife to whom I am totally committed. I owe her a lot.

It didn't take me long to make up my mind. I had dealt with this firm three or four times before, and they knew me only in a professional capacity. It's my nature to be somewhat stoic, although I have been known to show a sardonic wit now and then. I always come across as all-business, though, meaning: Let us all do what we came here to do and go on to something else. Perhaps they thought that I would deviate from my business persona and fall to my knees because of a lewd suggestion or two. I felt as if I was in a theatre of the absurd. I could hardly contain myself, I was laughing so hard. The look on her face showed me she wasn't overly amused at my reaction. When a woman makes a good honest proposal, she expects a favorable reply. When I finally composed myself, my response was, "I'll stick to the $18,500 offer and maybe you ought to consider cutting your fee." I wasn't going to compromise myself and become somebody's fool.

I considered bringing the matter to the attention of the ARDC. I also thought about complaining to the Chicago and Illinois Bar Associations as well. After some reflection, I realized that reporting it would only result in a big flat denial on the firm's part. Actually, it would have been a great test case for sexual harassment. I happen to believe that a heterosexual male cannot be sexually harassed unless ten women kidnap him, tie him up, and force him to perform sexual acts over and over. Some guys might be offended by my point of view, I suppose. In truth, I was quite flattered, and I enjoyed the diversion from what I thought was going to be a routine workday. These diversions and perversions make the banal nature of routine take a back seat for a little while! By refusing to join in their little game of deception, I put the onus back on them. They took a big chance and lost. I settled the case for $18,500 and sauntered away with a sack full of fond memories.

Hell Hath No Fury

I had a dispute with a female adjuster who worked for a well-known insurance company. Her company had insured a building where a tenant had fallen on a wet floor, and my principal had the insurance on the building's cleaning service. Because I thought it was right, I pressed very hard for her company to contribute to the settlement for the injured party. She refused on the basis that the cleaning service had made the building an additional insured on the cleaning service's liability policy. We did not indemnify the building for their negligence, only for the cleaning service's negligence. It was my position that it was the building that had failed to warn the tenants that the cleaning service would be mopping the floors between 1:00 a.m. and 5:30 a.m.

A Mr. Ben Pickett was visiting a very old friend at 3:00 a.m. He'd come off the elevator on the basement level and was on his way to his car when he slipped and fell on the wet floor. He injured his hip, but didn't break any bones. There were warning signs posted, but they weren't up in the exact location where he'd exited the elevator. There was a bank of four elevators, and signs did not appear by each and every door. I would venture to say that most everyone in the building knew when the cleaning service mopped. Regardless, I thought I had an excellent argument.

The woman I was arguing with met me at the attorney's office when we interviewed the claimant. After the statement was complete, I went after her, and I did so in front of the attorney so that he might put some pressure on, too. The trouble was, she had a terribly annoying and kind of condescending way about her. I gave her a double-barreled ration of derision, and I'm not sorry about it. Some people in our business ignore the art of making settlements. Compromise is the essence of getting the job done. I have always been very loyal to the people who pay me, and when I feel I'm right about an idea that could potentially reduce their exposure to a claim, I will fight vehemently for them. Sometimes, the fight is more fun when your adversary piques your fighting spirit.

Even after the client left and the attorney walked down the street with us, we were still going at it. In front of the claimant attorney she called me a "little pipsqueak, leprechaun, Irish bastard," and told me I wasn't fit to be in the professional business of insurance. First of all, I'm not all that diminutive! I really raised her ire when I responded that, "Compared to you, I'm a pygmy, but you ought not to throw your weight around because it is unbecoming of a lady!" She blurted out, "I ought to beat your ass!" Just before she walked away, a man approached us and asked if I needed help or if he should call for the police. I replied, "Thanks for your concern, but I think I can handle this."

I had to pull over to the side of the road a couple of times on the way back to my office because I was laughing so hard. She quit her job a week later. Her supervisor called me and told me confidentially that she thought the woman was a hothead. Everyone in the office was furious with her. As a way of apologizing, I was given $10,000 to play with to settle the case.

CHAPTER 10: THE GOOD, THE BAD, THE UGLY AND THE BIZARRE

The Good: Fessing Up

Lest you get the impression that my professional life is full of claimants who are sordid and tainted with filth, deception and avarice, allow me to acknowledge a woman who was once overpaid in the amount of $5,000--she returned the check and asked for the right amount. Then there was the lady, who under duress from my intense questioning about a rental car in her possession that was subsequently involved in an accident, came to see the light.

Initially, she tried to persuade me that her rental car had been stolen. She had even filed a stolen vehicle report with the Chicago Police. Although it certainly isn't more serious than a misdemeanor to file a false report with a police agency, the woman completely broke down as I peppered her with questions. I believe she was well aware that I wasn't buying her story. The full story came out in spurts: she had lied about the car being stolen from a gas station while she'd been in a phone booth; she said she had left the engine running because she'd only been five feet from the car. Then, all of a sudden, her story jumped to that of an unknown African-American male in his late teens or early 20s jumping into the car and driving away.

When verbal pressure was brought to bear upon her more forcefully, she broke down and told the truth. None of the major rental car companies rent to a person under the age of 25. The way around this limitation is for a parent or an adult friend to rent the vehicle and give permission to the minor to drive it. This woman had rented the vehicle for her son to use, and he'd given it to a friend, who, in turn, had given it to yet another friend. Illinois is a permissive-use state, meaning case law says that that's all right. However, permission granted from a friend of a friend of a friend doesn't cut it. The important thing is that we had discovered the truth, even if we'd made the woman cry doing it. It's amazing how much helpful information one can glean just by asking the right questions.

Another fellow —a company president I worked with had recovered more than $50,000 in tools and equipment an employee had stolen. His company had received a sizable payment from the insurance company to address this loss. A theft report was made, but the police had no leads. Then, it was discovered that a brother-in-law of the plant superintendent had taken the tools and equipment and had made the deadly but common error of telling someone in a bar. Word got back to the company while the thief waffled about whether to keep the items himself or to try to sell them underground. The thief returned the items. In the end, a very enlightened individual, the company president, did the honorable thing and returned all of the money to the insurance company.

I must give credit where credit is due: on some rare occasions, when I have presented a settlement offer, people have actually told me it is too much. I made a settlement offer to a man who only wanted his medical and nothing more. He signed a release form and took a check for $500 above his medical bills. He mailed me a check for $500, which I passed onto the insurance company. This was a rare occurrence indeed. It demonstrates, though, that not everyone is driven by greed.

An Almost Forgotten Faux Pas

Just before the two-year statute of limitations ran out, I found a fellow who had been the proximate cause of an accident. Since he had employed a major insurance carrier known for paying their claims, I was able to induce the company to pay for the majority of the claim with a little assistance from my principal.

In this case, a man named Robert Price had made an illegal U-turn, which had in turn precipitated a rear-end collision behind him. My principal insured the guy in the striking vehicle. Because the man who had made the U-turn had caused our insured to rear-end the car in front of him, the insurance carrier thought they could get their money back from the insurance carrier for the man who made the u-turn, because that driver had caused the accident in the first place. The occupants of that lead vehicle had more than $10,000 in property damage, and both parties had suffered soft tissue neck and back strains requiring multiple doctor visits, physical therapy and lost time from work. The entire case settled for $25,000.

Why everyone had waited so long to take action was beyond me. No one had even bothered to find the man who had caused the accident—he had been identified on the police report by his license plate number, but not his name. He was clearly at fault, though, and the police officer who had shown up on the scene should have issued him a ticket at least, because he had slowed down dramatically and suddenly, not giving the people in the car behind him time to react. He had, in effect, gotten away scot-free: his own vehicle was untouched. Someone had written down his plate number, but the police did not act on the information. The man didn't exactly flee.

When I was asked to step in, I had a source run the plate. From there, things were quite simple. I didn't have a current phone number for him, so one night I attempted to make a cold call on him in person. It seemed as if he was almost expecting me, which I knew was impossible. The incident had occurred two years before I showed up on his doorstep! When I introduced myself and began to ask him questions, he didn't try to deny any-thing, and he didn't argue about what had happened. He was, in fact, very apologetic, and he promised to contact his carrier the very next day. Though he didn't express himself in so many words, the look on his face was highly revealing. It told me that he knew he'd be held accountable in some way, someday. He could have been proactive about the matter; he could have assuaged his conscience by reporting the incident to his carrier; he could have ended the suspense long ago by following through, but he'd chosen to play the odds instead and he'd lost.

The ramifications were not severe—there was no threat of incarceration or public humiliation. I couldn't help but think, though, that Mr. Price somehow knew that on a foggy night in the future, a stranger would show up on his doorstep… not that I'm particularly ferocious or foreboding. Had those two years of uncertainty been worth it for him? It made me consider people who had done the unthinkable: war crimes or the murder of a spouse, disguised as a suicide. Is guilt a relative feeling? Did it matter what the consequences would eventually be? Wasn't it just always easier to deal with any situation and face the fear like a man? Imagine the waiting and anticipation, the restless nights, that nagging feeling eating away at your insides. Even Mr. Price, guilty of what might be considered a minor infraction, had experienced his own brand of agony. He hadn't lost his physical freedom, but his mind had been shackled for two long years.

The Bad: Fire and Brimstone

Another case involved a fire on the southside. A woman, her son, and her boyfriend lived in a frame building that had been converted into apartments. They lived on the second floor in the back. In July of 1982, on a typical, sultry, hot Sunday afternoon, she and her boyfriend had gotten into a violent argument, with physical and verbal abuse meted out from both parties. They had consumed a generic version of Southern Comfort—almost a quart bottle —and practically all of the liquor had been consumed by the time the argument had gotten out of hand.

In a fury, the female had threatened to set the building on fire. At first, her boyfriend had dismissed her rants. Then, while he was in the bathroom, she had torched the curtains in the dining room and kitchen. He'd come out, grabbed her son, and rushed out the backdoor. The building began to go up quickly—explosively. With her boyfriend on the second floor porch steps, pleading with her to come out, she'd stayed in the kitchen, shouting profanities out the window. Then she'd hid in a bedroom closet and locked the door. By the time the fire department broke down the door, she had suffered second- and third-degree burns over most of her face and body. Some people in the building had suffered mild smoke inhalation, but no one except for the arsonist had been seriously injured.

Even though the owner had reported that the fire was no accident, the insurance carrier wanted an investigation. Rumors from around the neighborhood were running rampant that the fire had not, in fact, been started by an individual, but had been electrical in nature. The Chicago Police bomb and arson squad made a thorough investigation.

The only way fire department reports could be obtained was by subpoena, but reports could be read in the department office. I brought a tape recorder, read the report aloud, and had it transcribed. The only way I could secure the confidential police report was to find a connection that would be willing to provide me with it under the table. Fortunately, the owner of the building had a brother who was a district commander with the Chicago Police. He cooperated with us—the cost was a dozen. Molitor golf balls.

The conclusion of both reports was that the fire had been deliberately set. Both reports read as follows: "The fire was deliberately set as a result of domestic dispute." I felt like I had a feather in my hat--I had provided classified information. "Heavy drinking was involved," the report added. I continued the investigation by interviewing several people who had lived at the destroyed building. I heard ten different stories.

The boyfriend tried like hell to skirt the question of how the fire had started. I read him the police report and he cracked. Ten weeks after the fire, I tracked down the fire starter herself. She had just left the burn unit at the University of Chicago. I went to visit her at the hospital earlier, but they would not let me see her. When I saw her, she was wrapped up with gauze and I could smell her burned flesh. The court reporter I was with was shaken. The situation was extremely uncomfortable and I really wanted nothing more than to get out of there.

She mumbled and was very difficult to understand. After some gentle prodding on my part, she told me the whole, true story. Frankly, I was speechless. She wondered if the insurance company would consider giving her a settlement. She needed about $2,500 to help get back on her feet. I told her point blank that the insurance company would never consider giving her a hot cent. She was very lucky not to be prosecuted.

Bad Faith Issues

I have utilized many different approaches in resolving matters. I negotiated with a law firm for over three months to settle a 15-year-old African-American girl's injury which had resulted in a keloid scaranodular linear mass of hyperplastic scar tissue on her right shin. She'd been hit while waiting at a bus stop by a driver who had run amok. In 10-degree weather, she'd been with her 8-month-old brother. Hard to believe that their mother had even allowed her to take the baby outside in that type of weather, using public transportation to go home in the dark.

We met in the attorney's office. Her scar was highly visible, and plastic surgery probably wasn't going to help very much. I politely asked her to go to the ladies' room twice to clean it up so I could photograph it properly. My message was designed more for the client than for the attorney: I was trying to point out that the scar really wasn't as bad as they were claiming. They asked for the policy limit of $100,000, and we settled for $71,000. The attorney had the case probated, and the judge approved the settlement, which was structured in the sense that the insurance company bought an annuity so that all the money was not paid up front. The case was probated so that the girl's parents wouldn't be able to spend the money at will without some direction from the court. The idea was to make sure that she would have money for her college education, at least. The annuity provided for that. The attorney took 33 percent of the settlement, and the rest of the $71,000 went toward buying the annuity after the medical bills were paid. The young lady realized an additional $21,000 through the interest, that was paid out by the annuity.

The negotiations took a protracted period of time because the liens involved had to be adjudicated. It also took a while for the attorney to embrace the notion that he wasn't going to receive the policy limit. He kept bringing up the issue of bad faith. "Bad faith" happens when a carrier won't pay the policy limit even when they know that the case is worth that much, or considerably more, than the policy limit. The carrier simply refuses to settle. The case involving the scar on the girl's leg was not a bad faith situation, though, because of many factors.

The scar represented a disfigurement, but it wasn't on her face. It was also apparent that she wasn't going to be a beauty queen or a movie star in the first place. She was significantly overweight, and her medical bills were not more than $7,500. There were no lost earnings. The jury verdict reporter highlighted several examples of these same types of cases showing a range of value nowhere near $100,000. It was more than an equitable settlement, and the attorney knew it. Instead, they continued to hold out for a settlement of $75,000 to $80,000, which was the figure they had in mind going into the negotiations.

Family Matters: Man Can Not Live on Bread Alone

I call 1985 . a difficult year. As a company, we had to make a lot of transitions. I worked out of my home until June of 1985, when my first child was almost 2 years old. With a wild child making toy planes out of my papers, I sublet an office. My one stable business source was preparing to move out of the down-town area, and I could sense they wouldn't be using us much longer. I found a new replacement for them and cultivated that prospect. With major effort and grind it out excellence, though, 1986 business prospects looked very promising. After my success with an aforementioned brain damage caper, the defendant's law firm referred me to yet another law firm who hired me.

The wife of an eccentric but unusually talented man had hired this attorney to prove that her husband was incapable of handling his own hard-earned money. In other words, the family was afraid that he was going to squander their inheritance. The colossal battle had been raging for five years. The woman's lawyer had been successful in that the court had granted an injunction which took the man's control of his money away, at least temporarily. The reasoning was that he was truly unstable. My task was to prove that he was, as we Americans say, fuckin' nuts.

The gentleman in question owned a very well-known bakery in Chicago, whose predominant product was a popular name-brand bread sold in large volume in the city's grocery stores. He had built the empire with his younger brother. Now, his wish was to turn his house into a museum, and he was very outspoken about his desire to disinherit his family. By the time his family began trying to prove him incompetent, he had retired, and was living high off the hog with his wife in a 20-room mansion in an affluent suburb. He had five vehicles from which to choose, and a chauffeur at his disposal, day or night. Now, though, he was feeling very resentful indeed about his wife and her intentions, yet they still cohabitated together. In every other sense of the word, they were estranged, living in separate wings and not speaking. Nor would he speak to his children, as he felt they were part of the conspiracy. He was right. After the injunction, he also fought with his brother (sometimes on the sidewalk in front of the bakery) because he assumed his brother was in cahoots with the family.

Prior to the injunction, the money was being spent at a brisk pace. According to the information we were able to gather, the man was suffering from manic depression and, in fact, he exhibited several of the disorder's symptoms. He also apparently eschewed taking his medication. Compulsion is a byproduct of depression, and his particular compulsion was antiques. He'd never met a picture frame or wrought-iron plant holder he didn't insist upon owning.

I decided that his ex–chauffeurs would be a good starting point to determine what this man was really like. After the injunction, he had retained his command of five vehicles for use on a regular basis, the employ of a chauffeur, and a $600 a week allowance. It immediately occurred to me that perhaps lie wasn't as unstable as I'd assumed. At the age of 69, his prerequisites for a chauffeur was that she be female, attractive, and under the age of 22. All of the chauffeurs I interviewed were quite beautiful. Because they were no longer under his employ, they spoke freely about the man and his escapades. He had never made a pass at any of the women, but none had lasted longer than a month. One of the women was a real knockout—she was the one who gave me the most information. She related the story of an argument she'd witnessed between the man and his younger brother where they had almost come to blows outside their corporate headquarters.

Our bakery owner's daily routine had been to drive all over the Chicago area, browsing for items in antique stores. After the injunction, though, he was on a budget. Soon, he began putting numerous items on layaway, too many to even count. I found out that he had nine storage lockers strategically placed around the Chicago metropolitan area full of antiques----some quite valuable, including both curios and unadulterated, unmitigated junk.

The attorney fees for the case were outrageous, and the legal fiasco had been dragged out over a period of two and a half years. Finally, a settlement was forged: the family would end up with $8 million in cash and securities. His wife moved out, and he retained his house in the suburbs of Chicago, along with $8 million in assets that were part of the estate. The value of the remainder of the estate was put in escrow. The man died just six months after the settlement was consummated.

Missing Links

In 1986, I received a useful referral from the same attorney I'd worked with on the bakery owner's case. The referral was for another attorney who had a very strained relationship with his son, who had been missing for several months. I was hired to try and find him. I worked on this case for nearly four months and couldn't get so much as a sniff of the kid despite some promising resources with which to work. I decided to collaborate with a former homicide detective, and we gathered dental records and fingerprints, which had been taken when he'd been arrested in Wisconsin for disturbing the peace and public drunkenness ten years before. We searched a national database, and we made con-tact with the FBI as well. I must have questioned more than a hundred people trying to find the young fellow.

In spite of their difficult relationship, the kid's father had bought him a seat on the Mercantile Exchange, but he'd been ejected, losing the seat along with a fair amount of money. He was a classic underachiever. As it turned out, he had later become involved in a number of real estate transactions with some rather questionable individuals who were buying tax delinquent properties and fixing them up for resale. About a year after the son had turned up missing, an acquaintance of his reported to me that he'd seen him walking on an overpass traversing the Kennedy Expressway at Addison. My first instinct was that he was being disingenuous.

In the past, the boy's father, my client, had apparently ridden his son hard about his various failures. The kid's mother was deceased, and the relationship between the two men could be described as tepid at best. Dad even admitted that he may have been too strident with his son, who had a drinking problem, and perhaps a drug problem as well. The apartment he lived in had clearly been abandoned. It looked as if he had simply left for work one day and never returned. The place was filthy, with clothing, dishes, and beer bottles strewn everywhere.

My own gut theory was that he was dead and buried some-where, possibly at the bottom of the Chicago River. The sense I'd gotten from talking to his business associates was that he had no real friends, and that he could be very annoying. The possible scenarios were endless. Personally, I'd be hard pressed to end anyone's life, even though I admit I've become somewhat jaded over the years. I just can't imagine being angry or spiteful enough to liquidate a human being for any reason. Nonetheless, my instincts told me that's how this kid had met his maker. I didn't give up, though. I went to halfway houses, shelters for the homeless, cheap hotels, and lower Wacker Drive and the area around the Maxwell Street market. Even with all the strain between father and son, Dad was very worried. In fact, his guilt was palpable.

A couple of months later, I got a call from a medical examiner's office. They had a guy that resembled the kid's description. Apparently, the deceased had made the fatal mistake of positioning himself under a truck's back wheels while the truck was stopped at a light on the northwest side of Chicago. When the truck started to move forward, it had crushed the man's skull, killing him instantly. It was a gruesome sight, and I couldn't tell if it was the subject just by looking at his mangled head, though he had red hair and the same height and build. Later, the fingerprints and dental records showed no match. Luckily, I hadn't yet called his father. I didn't want to alarm him unnecessarily.

After a year of very thorough local investigation, along with a national search, I was unable to find any leads. I contacted the father and told him I had done everything I could possibly do, and then I suggested that the Chicago Police should take a more active role. Curiously, the man was reluctant to follow that particular path. In fact, the Chicago Police already had a missing person's report out on our subject, but because of severe budget constraints, they had done virtually nothing. My thought was to convince the police, with the father's blessing, to treat the case as one of foul play similar to the Helen Vorees Brach case, in which the Brach Candy heiress was discovered missing in 1977. Truth be told, though, neither the boy's father nor I were overly confident that the police would pull out all the stops.

Five years later, an investigator came to my office. Operating under the request of the father, he was still looking for our subject. Five years later, no other details had been uncovered. Had the boy simply up and disappeared? The odds of his being alive in a new place, perhaps with a new lifestyle and identity, were remote at best. All I could offer after that period of time was my profound empathy.

The Ugly: Drunk and Nasty

A jury in the circuit court of Cook County, in deciding a law division case, awarded a despicable character $119,000 for an alleged fall he took down the common front stairway of his apartment building. Brad Melzer testified and convinced the jury that he had suffered a herniated disk at L4-5 as a result of his fall. He said that the stairway had inadequate lighting, and a hole in one of the steps had caused the carpeting covering that step to loosen. We were never able to find anyone who had heard or seen the fall. The facts of the case suggested that there were no complaints about the stairway previously.

Brad Melzer was an electrician working for an electrical contractor. He didn't work very often, and that was by choice. I suspected that he had actually created the hole in the steps him-self. Unfortunately, the building management did not provide a regular maintenance man who might have spotted the problem before anyone could fall. It really bothered me that this fellow cashed in. I thought, of all people, he didn't deserve a dime.

The building had been neglected to some degree. There wasn't much attention paid to details such as keeping the hall-ways and stairways clean. Common areas are an important responsibility for a building owner to maintain and keep clean—there is no doubt. Photographs of the loose step were provided by the plaintiff, and the insured didn't have any record, voucher, or a cancelled check to show that the step had been repaired—the insured would have to hire someone to repair it. In fact, the building owner should have had a resident designated as the caretaker, but did not even have that type of arrangement. In effect, the insured was a clay pigeon, primed for a lawsuit of this type.

Melzer possessed a bully mentality which manifested itself both verbally and physically. He was certainly an alcoholic if his two girlfriends could be believed. When he was intoxicated, his cruelty was manifested repeatedly. Both defense counsel and I had a suspicion that he hadn't fallen down the stairs at all. He had created that illusion. We thought he'd been hurt working in the construction trade as an electrician, although there were no records supporting that he had been involved in any accident on a job. It also occurred to us that he had been in an altercation with one or more combatants. Another theory was that he had been physically pummeled in a bar fight. Obviously, we couldn't find any record of that.

Melzer had gone to the hospital two days after the "accident" We felt that was quite a tip-off of chicanery right there. The hospital admission summary stated that he'd fallen down the common stairway in his building. I surmised that the more simple explanation was that he'd indeed fallen down the stairway, but it was because he was so drunk, he had no idea if he was going or coming. The factor of inadequate lighting, the broken step and loose carpeting, if legitimate, were points in his favor to making a successful claim, though. We had some hurdles to overcome from a defense standpoint because of those problems. We had to find something that would damage his credibility. A possibility was that he'd told one of his battered girlfriends that lie hadn't fallen down the stairs but that he'd injured his back at work while lifting something heavy.

I made contact with two of his ex-girlfriends. They wanted, in the worst way, to expose him for the bad actor he was, but neither one was enthusiastic about coming forward for fear of reprisal. One even had a protective order against him, but she didn't think for a minute that it would stop him from killing her if she thwarted his plans. Her help on the case would have been confined to denigrating his character anyway, because she had no firsthand information about where he'd fallen or whether he'd fallen at all. He'd beaten her up several times during a six- month span when they'd been together. Every time, he'd been soused. I know, because I secured the arrest records on this fellow. He'd been arrested for battery five times, yet he'd never been convicted. The women he'd assaulted would not testify against him.

I spent over six months trying to convince the two ex-girl-friends to come forward and testify. They were both terrified of what he might do if he found out that they were trying to burst his bubble. I even tried to convince the woman who did not have a protective order to seek one. The defense attorney agreed to put the paperwork together—we both hoped that if she had some assurance that the consequences were serious if he laid a finger on her, she'd cooperate. With a protective order, he surely would do significant jail time if he harmed one of them. A new stalking measure had recently been entered into law that had some serious bite to it.

One afternoon, I met with the girlfriend who had been present when Melzer had made the admission that he hadn't fallen down the stairs. Her story was horrific. He'd beaten her bloody one night, grabbing her hair and dragging her across the living room floor, out the door, and down the front steps. One night after they'd made love, and while he was pretty well gone, he'd admitted to getting hurt at work. The other battered ex-mate had no such information. These two women had become friends in a strange way—they felt a special kinship because of their shared experiences with this lunatic.

On another day, I met with both of them at a north side restaurant, but I couldn't convince either of them to testify. I told them to think about it long and hard. Without their testimony, especially the woman who'd been dragged by the hair, we could never hope to cast a shadow on him and put some meaningful doubt in the minds of the jury members. There was even some speculation that one of the women, the one with the protective order, would never be allowed to testify as she had nothing to say about the accident itself.

The case went to trial and the plaintiff attorney cleaned up his client from a physical standpoint. Melzer actually came across fairly well; he really knew how to play the game. Though the rules of evidence limit the introduction of certain types of information, the trial attorney wanted fervently to besmirch Melzer's character and show the court what a bad guy he was, but the judge wouldn't let certain items about his slap-happy past into evidence. There were no convictions, and it was decided that the battery charge revelations did not have any bearing or connection with his fall. Neither woman testified against him, and with no one to dispute the facts on how he'd injured his back, he received a hell of a nice chunk of change. Walking out of court, he had the smug look of a lucky victor.

Personally, I figured he'd eventually run out of good fortune and mouth off to the wrong person, creating a buzz-saw effect he couldn't deflect. This logic, whether true or not, took away some of the sting.

The Bizarre: Mirth Central

Not every situation an adjuster faces dwells on calamity. The woman I had once had the pleasure of meeting with the mouthful of saliva and strategically missing teeth—the one who had used her newspaper as a bludgeon---certainly fits that bill. Her tirade had only lasted 15 to 30 seconds, and had really taken the edge off for her son and his claim. Her son had been mad as hell about being thrown 30 feet after crashing through a windshield. Within hours of that poignant incident, though, I had been able to reflect back at how incredibly hilarious it had been. It was akin to something you'd see in a skit on the Red Skelton or Carol Burnett show. No one had been hurt, but the surreal and comedic characteristics of the incident had made it a very memorable one. For me, it brought to mind the old Soupy Sales routine, Black Fang and White Tooth.

Another rather amusing situation centered around a large black woman named Birdie McSwain, who weighed well over 250 pounds. Birdie was at a downtown hotel attending a speech given by a famous bishop from Africa in a banquet hall with 2,000 people. The bishop had a reputation as a captivating speaker. When Birdie sat down on her folding chair, it immediately collapsed and she bruised her ribs and hit her head. The insurance company for the chair's manufacturer demanded that Birdie be interviewed, and her attorney, against his better judgment, submitted. Having been hired by the insurance company, I was the interviewer, and I wrote her answers in longhand on a sheet of legal paper, which she later signed. When I arrived at the injury interrogation portion of the interview, I asked Birdie about her rib cage. She volunteered that there was still some discoloration in her left rib cage area. That's when I made the mistake of asking her if she had any photographs. I certainly wasn't prepared for her response, nor was her attorney.

Before we could make any protestations, Birdie rose from her chair and began to remove her jewelry. To my amusement, it appeared as if her clothing would be coming off next. I told her it was unnecessary, but as she pulled her dress over her head, she said, "I insist! And you ain't seen nothing yet!" I looked over at the attorney. He appeared to be in shock initially, but he was now smiling. Birdie continued her strip tease to the point where she was down to some type of corset, billows of fatty tissue spilling over everywhere. I had to give her credit: she had a decidedly uninhibited nature. Her bruises were clearly evident, and I went so far as to take a photo myself, but up close enough to leave the rest of her unclad body out of the shot. The carrier chuckled out loud when I handed in my report. They liked the pictures. In retrospect, I thank God the attorney was there as my witness. Imagine if I'd been forced to explain to authorities that I hadn't coerced Birdie to get naked!

Indoor Swimming

Picture a 700-unit high-rise building in a decent neighborhood. Now imagine if a tenant on the 18th floor decided to purchase and install a three-foot deep swimming pool in their apartment. You can probably guess what happened next: the liner for the pool sprung a leak and water seeped through the floor to the vacant apartment below, causing water damage. No one even knew until some painters came in to fix up the lower apartment for a new lease. The imaginative tenants with aquatic leanings were summarily dismissed from the building for conduct unbecoming to any building-dweller with any common sense. The apartments on the 15th and 16th floors had also sustained water damage, but nothing of major proportions.

Hair Today, Gone Tomorrow

Any man who has known a woman intimately knows that hair is cause for great concern and sometimes unbridled angst. In some instances, affinity with a certain hairstyle lasts as long as the cycle of one full moon to another. Some women change their coiffure as many as four or five times a year. Talk about a recession-proof business! Women spend inordinate amounts of money to cut, color, style and shape their hair. For me, at least, priorities seem to be skewed when one spends so much time, effort and money worrying about their hair. Some of this misdirected energy could be spent enjoying the outdoors or learning something new.

Men certainly have their own idiosyncrasies that women perceive as being equally absurd. However, two cases come to mind regarding hair coloring and hair straightening. The first case involved a woman who was experimenting with permanent hair coloring at home for a least a year. Her hair had become more and more brittle. I suspect she was overdoing the hair coloring, to say the least. She finally gave up and went to a salon, desperate for a miracle. As many salons do, this one's name reflected the proprietor's first name and middle name: David Paul. Her hair was four different shades of orange. The salon should have turned her away, advising her to wait for her hair to grow out. The next mistake they made was to allow an inexperienced hairdresser to attempt to fix her troubled tresses. The hairdresser was young, impressionable and easily bowled over. Because she possessed the unmitigated idealism only youth harbors, she thought she could do the impossible.

It was a two-step process. First, they applied the chemicals necessary for a permanent. Then they applied new hair color. The last thing this lady needed was more harsh chemicals on her scalp. Throughout, she complained that it felt like her scalp was on fire.

Unbeknownst to anyone, this woman with the mangled mane had some connections with the local media. A story about the incident was reported on the 10 o'clock news within days. The salon involved their insurance company, and my investigation revealed that the salon had used bad judgment—twice. They should have taken the time to think everything out before attempting to service her, and they shouldn't have assigned her the least experienced hairdresser in the salon. The salon wasn't entirely culpable, though, because this aggrieved straw-haired woman was very pushy. She had come in pleading for help. She was in "dire straits," she said. The hairdresser had felt great empathy for her. They should have just sold her a wig. In the end, it cost the insurance company $20,000 to clean up the toxic chemical spill on her scalp.

There is a very fancy salon on the Magnificent Mile in Chicago. The general manager there told me that they did about $12 million in gross receipts a year. This place was an assembly line for straightening, teasing, coloring and cutting. They called the hairdressers "associates," and had 20 of them working at any one particular time. A wide array of other services, from facials and massages to manicures, were available, and there was a large male clientele as well.

A young, professional, attractive African-American woman went to the hair salon primarily to have her hair cut and straightened, and they had used some very strong chemicals to achieve the desired result, including sodium hydroxide. When I inter-viewed two of the key "associates" regarding the plight of the injured party, we sat in the room where I would have been afraid to light a match because of the odor of the chemicals. I had a minor rash on the back of my left hand for a couple of days after having been there.

This woman's friend had given her a home permanent and had used peroxide to lighten her hair. In late March, she was told by her hairdresser not to have her hair straightened until June, but she just couldn't wait, so she made an appointment with another associate who was not familiar with her. Just to be safe, she made sure her regular associate had the day off. On that fateful day, the new associate noticed she had a permanent, but she went ahead anyway and applied the straightening chemical without asking any questions. She was inexperienced and eager to please. Over the next week, the woman's hair fell out in bunches. She contacted the salon, who took her in, and where her own hairdresser mildly chastised her. The woman was simply mortified, and even though she surely knew she had had a hand in the predicament, she raised a heck of a stink. The salon, trying to appease her, gave her a letter promising free services for a year.

I interviewed the woman in her office. She was very well spoken and had been getting legal advice from someone "behind the scenes" She told me that she just could not abide by the fact that it would take one and a half years for her hair to grow back to its former length.

When we finished the interview, she told me she was looking to resolve the matter by taking a cash settlement, which is exempt from income taxes. I asked what she had in mind. I was shocked—she answered that $300,000 would put her mind at ease. I immediately had to discern if she was serious or if she was shooting for the stars, so I told her that my principal would never consider such a ridiculous sum. I did agree to talk to the carrier, though. She faxed me a letter with her demand in writing, which was at my office before I made it back myself that day. A day later, I called and offered her $5,000. We negotiated back and forth, and she finally took $8,000, a far cry from her initial demand. During the two occasions when I met her, not even when I gave her the check, this attractive young lady, hair or no hair, never cracked a smile—not once.

Man's Country

Any person's preferred sexual orientation is none of my damn business, but I'll admit, life is hard enough being straight. I received a call from a customer one day asking if I would be willing to go to Man's Country, a club this possible client had just started to cover. At that point in my career, I wasn't yet established enough to turn down a case. There was a certain amount of intrigue on this one as well. In the wee hours of the morning, a patron of the club had fallen off a three-tiered platform and broken his wrist.

Man's Country was a gay conclave—kind of like a bathhouse without the water. This exclusive club required membership: to gain admittance to Man's Country, one had to pay a $5 entry fee to stay for the day (or evening), along with $2 for a locker and a fluffy terrycloth towel. The $5 fee covered one admittance for the day and a year's membership. The place was located on the north side of Chicago in an old movie theater. When I arrived, my contact turned out to be a guy with a clean-shaven head and a bushy mustache; he was shirtless but wore tight leather pants with bandoliers. He looked a little bit like Jesse Ventura. Mr. Clean explained the procedures thoroughly and showed me where the accident had occurred.

The fellow who had fallen, Billy Magic, had been extremely intoxicated —the club allowed members to bring in their own beverages. Billy had been dancing with another chap and had forgotten that he was on a platform, four and a half feet above the floor, in the grand ballroom. The place was fairly dark even on an August day, and at least 20 couples were huddled together around the perimeter of the well-appointed space. I took photo-graphs; none of the couples so much as glanced at me.

Later, I was able to locate Billy's companion, who reluctantly related the salient facts. The hospital records I obtained indicated Billy's blood alcohol level had been 0.29, which is fairly well on the road to being really plastered. Currently in Illinois, if you register .08 or above, it is considered legally intoxicated.

A year later, I noticed that Man's Country was closed.

Strange Bedfellows

Imagine a bar called the "Glory Hole" A nice place to grab a brew after work, no? Forget about it! This establishment had an offbeat clientele, to say the least: not what you'd call a straight as an arrow crowd. The carrier I worked for at the time had insurance coverage on the building, and also the dram shop coverage, which is required by all businesses that allow customers to consume liquor on the premises. Dram coverage, for example, kicks in if a customer is, to put it mildly, "over served," gets behind the wheel of a car and then causes an injury to occur to another party. By law, the injured party has recourse against the establishment that "over served" the customer who caused the accident. What if a drunk individual becomes belligerent and hits someone over the head with a belt buckle?

Some people might have a difficult time conjuring up images of oddly, and often underdressed imbibing fools becoming bellicose in nature, or driving without any inhibitions or due care for their fellow human beings. It happens more often than one would imagine. Fortunately, I had the excellent luck of never having to visit the notorious Glory Hole after sundown, when its unique brand of clientele was out in full force. Instead, when I visited the place during the day; it looked downright seedy, utterly lacking in glamour, and it smelled to high heaven, but it was mercifully empty of revelers. Maybe, I thought to myself, the Glory Hole employed a dimly lit ambiance to prevent regurgitation from being an often-repeated occurrence.

The place, opened at 2:00 in the afternoon, was located a couple of blocks from the lake, just north of downtown Chicago. You could walk two and a half blocks to the east and find 5-million dollar homes sitting alongside a number of foreign consulates. I secretly hoped the Norweigan Charge d' Affaires would not be exploring his feminine side during my visit. I was there to do a job, and that job was to track down one of the bartenders who had been on duty on one fateful night. Only he no longer worked there.

The case I was investigating had started when a big bruiser and ex-con, Doug Armbruster, was inside the Glory Hole throwing back a few non-alcoholic drinks all by himself. His latest visit to the big house had been for armed robbery, and he'd gotten out of jail less than two weeks before the incident I was investigating had occurred. From the profile I had on him, I had a feeling he had a strong desire to return to his former barred residence. Maybe he just couldn't cope on the outside. Armbruster was reported to have been wearing a white T-shirt, black boots, and jeans with the cuffs rolled up. He reportedly also wore a big, wide, black belt with a very heavy buckle. His head was clean shaven.

I still had one vexing question, and that was the big bruiser's sexual preference. My guess was that he was a latent homosexual with a heavy dose of schizophrenic tendencies; he was paranoid and maniacal with sociopath tendencies as well. I knew this because he'd beaten the crap out of a guy who had played the submissive role in a gay relationship who had been sitting next to him in the Glory Hole one night. The effeminate fellow had been minding his own business, waiting for his partner, when Armbruster had blown a gasket and pummeled him into unconsciousness. His offensive sin?

He'd made the mistake of attempting to make some small talk with the ex-con. The big bruiser had stomped the guy at least ten times with his right boot heel, but the belt buckle had been the most prominent weapon used. The victim had been hit once in the face and once on the back of the head while he was writhing on the floor in excruciating pain. No one had even tried to intervene. When he was satiated, the violent creep had casually walked out of the bar, and the police had picked him up a few blocks away in another bar where he was enjoying a drink of soda water as if nothing had happened

In truth, the victim was fortunate to be alive. He recovered fairly well, but he'd soon come to the decision that suing the Glory Hole was in order as they had allegedly provided the attacker with copious amounts of liquor. In my mind, however, there was something amiss. When he'd been picked up by the cops, he'd been drinking seltzer water. The bartender at the Glory Hole claimed he hadn't been drinking alcohol prior to the beating. Apparently, Doug Armbruster didn't need alcohol to fuel his rage—he was a nut all on his own.

One of the counts in the lawsuit addressed the problem of improper security at the bar, so the business and building's owner were also being sued. I met with him one night at his apartment. I rely on gut instinct a lot in my line of work, and my first impression of this guy was that he appeared to be running some kind of a sting operation in conjunction with the police, or with some other law enforcement agency like the FBI. To my amazement, he had at least 20 people in his home working on computers and sophisticated communications equipment. The "staff" there had the undeniable smell of professional G-men. Or maybe it was a sophisticated drug ring or bookie concession, I wondered. Why had he asked me to meet him there'? Was this all a legitimate operation?

I immediately sensed that this building owner had a very contentious attitude regarding his tenant, and for some reason, he confided in me that he suffered from agoraphobia. Naturally, I was surprised when I saw him two weeks later in a bike shop down the street. He looked very relaxed, and he was talking, rather animatedly, to an attractive female. At the time, he didn't let on that he recognized me, and I returned the favor. Maybe his agoraphobia acted up only on certain days—like people who suffer when the pollen count is high.

The big bruiser ended up going back to the clink for a long stretch, but a 12-year sentence with good behavior could potentially spring him in less than seven. He'd surely end up back on the streets to perform his acts of terror again. How I wish some monsters like him could be incarcerated permanently.

Six months later, the defense attorney requested that I serve a subpoena to a fellow at the offices of a gay publication that had its modest publishing facility just down the street from the infamous Glory Hole. The owner of this newspaper, unbeknownst to the victim, had actually arrived at the bar while the victim was being mauled on that night months before. In fact, I believe he was the victim's lover and the man he'd been waiting for. Yet he'd never lifted a finger to save his pal. He made his feelings clear from the start - he didn't like the fact that he was being asked to testify. He was downright hostile, as a matter of fact. If a look could kill, I would have been six feet under right then and there.

I don't always find out the outcome of cases I work on, but in this one, the injured party received $128,000 in an out-of-court settlement. The general liability carrier for the bar paid the entire sum. The dram shop carrier paid nothing because it was demonstrated that Armbruster had not been drinking.

CHAPTER 11: HOW LOW WILL YOU Go?

Motor Queen

Running a successful small business is no picnic. There are many components that go into making such an endeavor viable. In any business, motivated people are the key. Monetary consideration is certainly important, but it doesn't end there. Working conditions are crucial as well. When employees are hired, especially those in management, they must be given enough latitude to do their job. There has to be trust--no one can work effectively with someone else looking over their shoulder. I have been running a small business for well over 20 years. Before that, I worked for a family business; the reason it didn't grow was that the owner was so involved in the small details, he couldn't see the big picture. Anyone who worked for him was considered a lackey because that was the way he treated them after the initial honeymoon period wore off.

I was involved in an investigation stemming from two allegations of wrongdoing by the management of a small regional auto parts business. This small company had the usual cover-ages from an insurance standpoint: they had a comprehensive general liability policy, which provides no coverage for claims made by employees for acts of wrongdoing by management such as libel, slander, or sexual harassment. They also had workers' compensation coverage, which did not address these issues either. Workers' compensation coverage protects the employer and the employee. It provides benefits for an employee injured during the course of his or her work, and in some instances, workers' compensation coverage provides benefits for employees who are victims of job- related stress. To provide coverage for wrongful termination or libel, slander, or sexual harassment, an employer has to purchase employer practices liability coverage.

In these times, when attorneys have devised a veritable cornucopia of new avenues to attack the legal system and make employers accountable for a whole host of rights violations, it becomes necessary to have this type of coverage. Sadly, many businesses, especially smaller ones, don't have it. The regional auto parts shop, however, did have this coverage, and at the time that the allegations came to light, they had 75 employees.

The workforce in general is a bubbling cauldron these days. Part of this is due to the fast-paced, cutthroat, capitalistic system that we embrace. The other consideration is one of basic civility. I happen to believe that excessive viewing of television, especially network prime-time programming, has facilitated a severe erosion of common decency and manners, even in the workplace. One of the key employees of this small business (but not an officer, nor a family member), decided to take the low road and go crooked. It was never proved conclusively, but a careful consideration of their books would reveal an inventory loss of more than $240,000. This employee never admitted to moving merchandise illegally, but eventually things came to a head and he was terminated. A police investigation followed. The employee was not arrested, but the authorities were very anxious to try and prove something against him; they were literally groping for documentation to prove that he was guilty, and he was questioned several times.

I urged the employer to gather the necessary paperwork, which demonstrated the inventory loss. Unfortunately, the employee had never been caught with inventory in his vehicle, or transporting inventory illegally. There was, however, much circumstantial evidence pointing to this individual as the guilty party. I soon learned that he was a master of jerry-rigging invoices. He had held the title of purchasing manager, so he was responsible for overseeing, ordering and purchasing inventory for all of the company's stores. One ploy was to transfer stock from one store to another by means of the computer, thereby creating confusion. In some instances, he would then transfer the inventory back to the store where it had come from in the first place. He also would take items and put them in his vehicle, ostensibly to take them to another store. The company had two trucks that moved 99 percent of the merchandise from store to store as needed. Several employees had knowledge of this unusual movement. What I eventually found out was that he was taking high ticket items and selling them to other stores, not connected to the business he actually worked for. Those other stores would then sell these items for cost, or in some instances, below cost. These items included fuel injectors, distributor caps and wiring.

About a month after he was let go, an attorney's lien arrived at his former employer's workplace, alleging that his character and good name had been besmirched and irreparably damaged. Furthermore, he alleged sexual harassment! His claim was that the president of the company, a female, had lifted up her skirt and said something to the effect of, "Get a load of this!" He claimed she had no underwear on. When I met the president of the company, and I had the opportunity to interview her extensively, I had to laugh. She was a tough cookie, and I wouldn't have been surprised if she actually had lifted her skirt, just to show this fellow how tough she was.

If this guy was guilty of masterminding the systematic and continued theft of inventory, then the slander/libel charges would not hold up. As far as sexual harassment is concerned, I surmised that the allegation had been thrown in to deflect attention away from his complicity in the loss of inventory. I also thought that there may have been another employee that was acting in concert with him.

The insurance carrier I worked for didn't have coverage for either allegation, so the matter was handled by sending a reservation of rights letter where the carrier stated that coverage was not guaranteed for any of the allegations, but the right was reserved to investigate the matter and decide coverage at a later date. I interviewed nine or ten people who worked for the company, including the 82-year-old founder who was since retired, but who still had a pretty good handle on events at the company. I also communicated on numerous occasions with the police.

An important figure in all of this was the company's chief financial officer. I called him the "keeper of the books and financial records." We communicated on several occasions, and I was convinced that with his documentation, and evidence provided by various employees, that the wrongful termination and libel/slander charge could be overcome. I told the carrier that the best defense was to see him arrested and indicted. The carrier wanted no part in pursuing it that vigorously. I urged the CFO to provide the police whatever they required in the form of paperwork. I suspect that because coverage was not forthcoming from my principal, that to keep a low profile was a prudent way to handle things. Let the employer practices-liability carrier worry about it, I thought.

In a larger company or corporation, the president would not have been so intimately involved in a matter of this ilk. But emotions were running hotter than a taxi in stop and go traffic in Manhattan. In a large company, in-house legal or security could have handled a problem like this. I wouldn't be surprised if some seemingly dicey things had been said to the ex-employee. Upper management would normally be involved in the decision-making, but they would have been insulated, whereas in the small company like the auto parts concern, there wasn't any layer of protection for upper management. The company was thrown into chaos over the whole affair, and I got the impression that they just wished it would go away. For me, it was a fascinating study of human emotions under duress. I sometimes lament the fact that I rarely see people when they are exuding positivity.

Swisher

In 1978, one of the largest hospitalization carriers in the United States had offices in downtown Chicago; they had multiple departments on several floors. There may have been 2,000 employees at their downtown location alone. I was asked to investigate a carnage that had taken place in the claims review department. A lady who was working there definitely lacked a "life of the party" personality; she was there to work, and she wasn't too friendly with the male staff. Consequently, they teased her mercilessly in a way that would make Senator Packwood look like a choir boy. She was, in fact, married to a minister.

The woman had an admittedly peculiar physical characteristic: when she walked, her derriere shook like a bowl of Jell-O. She wasn't unattractive, and she had a decent figure, but her rear end was, frankly, enormous. The teasing went on for months, and all the while her supervisor was aware of it. He did little to intervene. All of this transpired in the late 1970s—a time I characterize as the "age of litigation innocence" Nowadays, it seems that everyone has a heightened sense of what their rights are in the workplace, and many are poised to act if their rights are violated. Instead of the tolerant atmosphere of that time, there is now a profusion of sexual harassment claims in the workplace, and employers are being held accountable.

She did suffer silently for months, but this gal wasn't entirely innocent, considering what she did to retaliate. Her nickname was "Swisher," and she grew to hate the unsavory name just as a boy would react if he were called "Jane." I'm familiar with a football player whose real name is Norman, but he prefers to be called Boomer. As a matter of fact, he abhors the name Norman and insists on the alias.

I had a chance to interview "Swisher" before she was eventually sentenced for a horrendous crime. She related her misery and extreme discomfort to me, and said that the teasing had caused her to stop eating.

Furthermore, her hair had begun to fall out and she was not sleeping well. She described herself as a "pitiful wreck." After a full morning of very strong, vehement and intense harassment from one fellow in particular, the ringleader, who had a band of merry followers, she had finally snapped on that horrible day. Waiting by the elevator bank on the 18th floor, right before lunch, she just happened to have a razor blade with her. When the fellow passed by, she tried to cut his throat at the Adam's apple. She missed his jugular by a centimeter. The man didn't die, but the wound required 75 stitches. It smacked of premeditation.

Swisher was arrested, indicted and did jail time. She was actually very contrite when I met with her, though I made sure to keep my eye on her, just in case. I was fairly certain that she was not the type to commit random acts of violence to appease a blood- thirsty appetite; in a sense, she was a victim, too. I felt badly for her, though obviously she should not have resorted to such mayhem to solve the problem. She had, of course, lost her job, her freedom and her husband. In the late 1990s, she would have had an airtight case for suffering extreme exasperation in contradiction to any corporate policy prohibiting sexual harassment in the workplace. The ration of abuse she endured was so outrageous and heinous that the corporate coffers would have been more than slightly diminished if that corporation was self insured for dealing with this type of activity.

I characterize this tragedy as having two victims, not one. The lady who finally snapped had no prior history of violence, and she felt she had no one to confide in. She felt trapped, and she was afraid of quitting her job for fear of reprisal from her husband. I certainly don't condone what she did, but I surely understand why she did it. Money doesn't solve problems, but had this been 20 years later, the "teasing" probably wouldn't have been allowed. She would have made a figurative killing with a savvy attorney! I believe some clever people use sexual harassment as a weapon to find Easy Street, but this woman was truly a legitimate candidate who suffered enormous abuse.

More Than Meets the Eye

A golfing buddy of mine, Terry Esposito, is an attorney who does a lot of real estate closings. Terry referred a personal injury case to an attorney friend, Ralph Goodyear, whose specialty was personal injury cases.

Not knowing Goodyear, he and I engaged in a few testy conversations at first. We were kind of feeling each other out. He was somewhat abrasive, but after he realized that I wasn't a pushover, he calmed down. His client had been in a bad automobile accident, and had suffered the typical soft tissue injuries. He had been given conservative care, including a few doctor visits and diagnostic tests, and he had gone to the emergency room on the same day that the accident had occurred.

The issue that made this case different from a value stand-point was that the driver had been sprayed with glass, leaving him with scratches that had healed with no residuals, except that his right cornea was scratched. This event occurred well before laser surgery had been perfected, and the man was having problems with blurred vision and a watery eye. Apparently, an infection had ensued because his eye hadn't been cleansed thoroughly in the emergency room. The eye doctor reported in his notes that he hoped the condition would clear up in time with the proper medication, but he gave it a less than 50 percent chance. Surgery was an option, but the client was afraid.

I tried to settle the case. The woman who was acting as the claim handler at the insurance company was skeptical. I was given $27,500 to resolve it. I offered $22,500, and the attorney indicated that he was looking for more, $45,000. I negotiated with him over a period of three weeks; he finally came down to $30,000, and I went up to $26,000. The attorney, however, refused to budge from his $30,000 demand. I knew that if the carrier would give me an additional $1,500, I could get the attorney to cut his fee slightly and the case would settle. He had already threatened to send his client to a more renowned eye doctor, often used by defense attorneys to confirm a diagnosis, and I knew at that point that $29,000, or even $30,000, was a steal. This time, the carrier refused to budge.

The attorney immediately hired a well-known ophthalmologist who confirmed the diagnosis, and the case settled for $40,000 instead of $29,000. It left a bad taste in my mouth I had settled for $11,000 more than the case should have taken to resolve. At first, the attorney stuck to his $45,000 demand. Finally, he came down to $40,000 in the name of closure. I convinced him that for an extra $5,000, he would be doing everyone a disservice by filing suit and incurring tremendous expenses such as bringing in experts to testify, including the ophthalmologist. The claim handler who had refused to settle for $29,000 was rather sheepish when she called, asking me to please try and resolve the case for up to $40,000. If I'd known the woman a little better, I would have put the squeeze on her for the extra money, the $1,500 that would have brought us up to $29,000. Had she been wiser from the beginning, she would have saved her company $11,000.

It was, in fact, colossally stupid in my view, and I'd seen other cases mistreated in the same way. Second-guessers run rampant in this business, and I've often wondered why I've been hired to do a job, and then not given the latitude to complete it because of a lack of trust. I believe it reverts back to that archaic notion that claims people are the bad guys. Someone was bound to second-guess her, so she was going to second-guess me. Any settlement under $30,000 would have been a steal. I knew the case intimately, and my own instincts were the best suited to make sound judgments. I had informed intelligence that could have mitigated their costs.

Another case I dealt with involved a carrier who had created an environment where trust was a four- letter word. They used honest and smart people like me, but they didn't trust us to keep indemnity dollars at a minimum. The best-suited person to settle a case is the one who knows the file inside and out. An investigator employs different skills, as opposed to a negotiator, but there is always an overlap. Learning to be a crack negotiator is an acquired skill, and a skilled negotiator is always a good actor.

It's a lot easier to quantify expenses than indemnity dollars. Insurance companies don't pay the same amount of attention to holding down indemnity dollars or settlement proceeds as they do expenses. Both outlays come from the same till, and both. equally determine whether a property-casualty company is successful from a financial standpoint.

I had a situation where a carrier settled a case for $45,000 while I had a chance to settle it for $25,000. Authority to settle the case was not granted, because the file handler was inept and incompetent and couldn't pull the trigger. Talk about inertia!

The case involved a 16-year-old kid whose teeth had been smashed in an automobile accident. He needed six implants, which required a painful two-step surgery. Because of his age, the case had to be handled in probate court; but even with over $8,000 in medical expenses, or projected medical expenses, a judge clearly would have approved a $25,000 settlement. But the file handler would not listen to reason. She was incapable of making decisions. The value of the case went up when another attorney took over the case and convinced the court and the carrier handling the case that it was worth $45,000. The argument was that this young man was in for a lot of discomfort. Implant surgery is complicated and it hurts. All teeth couldn't be done at once—perhaps two in one sitting. That meant at least two visits to an oral surgeon, followed by a session with a dentist who would actually build the teeth and fit the prosthesis to the hard-ware already inserted in the jaw by the oral surgeon. In addition, implants are not permanent—they can last 20 years at best.

This was another egregious example of an insurance company employing incompetent people and entrusting them, rather than listening to the voice of experience. In essence, they were advocating an oft- repeated situation: if employees don't do things that conform to their ideology, it's okay. I became incensed time after time when some ignoramus would bust my chops for submitting an expense bill which they perceived to be inflated. They still have no idea how much we investigators and adjusters save them, because we provide information which helps them mitigate or deny claims. Secondly, as negotiators, we save them money because we know values instinctively. Good firms make assiduous efforts to justify repeated hiring. For more than 25 years, I have saved my clients well over $25 million. They have paid me a lot as well, but nothing approaching that figure.

CHAPTER 12: FINAL **THOUGHT**

Many of the cases discussed in this book concerning the insurance industry and situations that have arisen in various investigations would never find their expression in a report or letter for fear of discovery in the litigation process. I am referring to the plaintiff bar having subpoena power to secure such reports or letters. Once litigation ensues, reports and/or letters will be sent to the defense attorney, establishing attorney --client privilege. There are some ways to circumvent this, but it makes it more difficult for the plaintiff or co-defendant in a case to get their hands on classified documents. The carrier receives a copy of everything I send to the attorney. The carrier also pays my invoice. There is a cloak of protection.

That doesn't mean I would espouse crazy ideas or opinions in spite of that protection; I am very careful not to demean anyone; I am obliged to describe what kind of witness a per-son will make. If it is negative, I will report it verbally, so there is no written record. I was once told by an old, erudite claims genius to never tell a carrier in writing where coverage might be triggered, but that it is okay to say when coverage should not be afforded —never put the carrier in a position where they are locked into something.

When a claims professional makes a determination that there may not be coverage, the agent, the client, and the insured often don't understand, or refuse to try and understand, the reasons. It is almost as if we are not speaking the same language. Many times, these coverage issues affect the relationship between the insured and a good client or customer. In these instances, the claims professional becomes the bearer of bad news. This is another example of why people just don't want to deal with us--they think they should keep both hands in their pockets for fear of being fleeced.

It helps to be an effective communicator to ward off the pallor of distrust. I have often been involved in three-way conversations with an agent and an insured, principally to help the insured under-stand why an action is being taken, or to explain how a decision has been made by the carrier. As much as I have tried not to interfere with a relationship between an insured and a good customer, it is sometimes impossible not to ruffle some feathers.

Being on time, acting professionally, looking professional, and not making commitments I can't keep are essential. The last thing I want to do is meddle in a situation that is fragile at best. Many times, I have to meet with a good customer of an insured because the insured's employees have done something to cause damage to property, or the customer's employees are injured. In many instances, we can smooth things over and resolve these issues painlessly. The additional insured endorsement sometimes takes the sting out of the business relationship when the insured has his carrier name the client as an additional insured on the insured's policy. Then, if something happens, there is a better spirit of cooperation and less finger-pointing.

Over the years, my distrust of attorneys in the plaintiff bar has dissipated gradually. Lack of experience makes one crawl into a shell and become too distrustful and protective. The more experienced one becomes, the less paranoid one is, because concepts that were not obvious in the beginning can be seen coming from a long distance. I don't worry so much about the small, insignificant things that might obfuscate my mind and deter me from seeing the big scheme. It's often a chess game, and if you know all the moves in advance, you are less likely to make mistakes. When I deal with people I don't know, they usually test me to see if I am a pushover. Once we get past that, wariness commonly fades away and reasonable communication takes place.

When trying to accomplish anything in life, I can't emphasize enough the importance of embracing the spirit and art of compromise. This concept, when put into action, has helped resolve many vexing problems—ones that I never believed in a million years could be resolved. At first, the rhetoric and tone start out ugly and become highly contentious. Consequently, the parties are far apart. But when I use a little creativity, I even surprise myself. Problems that seemed hopeless at first are settled. I have always had great confidence that I can resolve anything if there are two willing par-ties. This is not a black- and- white world we live in. If someone continues doing things the same way and keeps getting the same results, one needs to find a different approach or face the same disappointments over and over. If someone works for an organization that handicaps its workforce by not giving them the latitude or authority to do a job properly, then one either has to leave, or anesthetize himself or herself to a lack of results and satisfaction of a job well done. I know so many people in my industry who never rise above this conundrum and I feel great empathy.

I mean no disrespect to those who have faced misfortune. I. do not intend to make light or poke fun at anyone. In the final analysis, I have been thrust into a re-active role, by nature of my calling, to attempt to sort out issues from an insurance claims perspective. I have not been called upon to save the world from evil or wrongdoing or misery, although there have been many times I wish I could snap my fingers and it would all go up in a cloud of smoke. I hope it is apparent that I haven't much sympathy or empathy for the cheaters and frauds of our little universe. The stories and personalities keep coming like a juggernaut, and will continue long after our generation entropy fighters are forgotten.